Mole

D0989035

Animal
Series editor: Jonathan Burt

Already published

Albatross Graham Barwell · *Ant* Charlotte Sleigh · *Ape* John Sorenson · *Badger* Daniel Heath Justice
Bat Tessa Laird · *Bear* Robert E. Bieder · *Beaver* Rachel Poliquin · *Bedbug* Klaus Reinhardt
Bee Claire Preston · *Beetle* Adam Dodd · *Bison* Desmond Morris · *Camel* Robert Irwin
Cat Katharine M. Rogers · *Chicken* Annie Potts · *Cockroach* Marion Copeland · *Cow* Hannah Velten
Crocodile Dan Wylie · *Crow* Boria Sax · *Deer* John Fletcher · *Dog* Susan McHugh · *Dolphin* Alan Rauch
Donkey Jill Bough · *Duck* Victoria de Rijke · *Eagle* Janine Rogers · *Eel* Richard Schweid
Elephant Dan Wylie · *Falcon* Helen Macdonald · *Flamingo* Caitlin R. Kight · *Fly* Steven Connor
Fox Martin Wallen · *Frog* Charlotte Sleigh · *Giraffe* Edgar Williams · *Goat* Joy Hinson
Goldfish Anna Marie Roos · *Gorilla* Ted Gott and Kathryn Weir · *Guinea Pig* Dorothy Yamamoto
Hare Simon Carnell · *Hedgehog* Hugh Warwick · *Hippopotamus* Edgar Williams · *Horse* Elaine Walker
Hyena Mikita Brottman · *Human* Charlotte Sleigh and Amanda Rees · *Jellyfish* Peter Williams
Kangaroo John Simons · *Kingfisher* Ildiko Szabo · *Leech* Robert G. W. Kirk and Neil Pemberton
Leopard Desmond Morris · *Lion* Deirdre Jackson · *Lizard* Boria Sax · *Llama* Helen Cowie
Lobster Richard J. Kin · *Mole* Steve Gronert Ellerhoff · *Monkey* Desmond Morris · *Moose* Kevin Jackson
Mosquito Richard Jones · *Moth* Matthew Gandy · *Mouse* Georgie Carroll · *Octopus* Richard Schweid
Ostrich Edgar Williams · *Otter* Daniel Allen · *Owl* Desmond Morris · *Oyster* Rebecca Stott
Parrot Paul Carter · *Peacock* Christine E. Jackson · *Pelican* Barbara Allen · *Penguin* Stephen Martin
Pig Brett Mizelle · *Pigeon* Barbara Allen · *Polar Bear* Margery Fee · *Rat* Jonathan Burt
Rhinoceros Kelly Enright · *Salmon* Peter Coates · *Sardine* Trevor Day · *Scorpion* Louise M. Pryke
Seal Victoria Dickenson · *Shark* Dean Crawford · *Sheep* Philip Armstrong · *Skunk* Alyce Miller
Snail Peter Williams · *Snake* Drake Stutesman · *Sparrow* Kim Todd · *Spider* Katarzyna and Sergiusz
Michalski · *Swallow* Angela Turner · *Swan* Peter Young · *Tiger* Susie Green · *Tortoise* Peter Young
Trout James Owen · *Vulture* Thom van Dooren · *Walrus* John Miller and Louise Miller
Wasp Richard Jones · *Whale* Joe Roman · *Wild Boar* Dorothy Yamamoto · *Wolf* Garry Marvin
Woodpecker Gerard Gorman · *Zebra* Christopher Plumb and Samuel Shaw

Mole

Steve Gronert Ellerhoff

REAKTION BOOKS

To Tom and Kay Ellerhoff

Published by
REAKTION BOOKS LTD
Unit 32, Waterside
44–48 Wharf Road
London N1 7UX, UK
www.reaktionbooks.co.uk

First published 2020
Copyright © Steve Gronert Ellerhoff 2020

All rights reserved

No part of this publication may be reproduced, stored in a retrieval
system or transmitted, in any form or by any means, electronic,
mechanical, photocopying, recording or otherwise, without the prior
permission of the publishers

Printed and bound in India by Replika Press Pvt. Ltd

A catalogue record for this book is available from the British Library

ISBN 978 1 78914 222 8

Contents

Foreword 7

1 Evolution 9

2 Nature 27

3 Scientific Study 53

4 Moles in Myth and Folklore 72

5 Allegorical Moles 98

6 Moles in Literary and Popular Culture 113

7 The Hunted Mole 158

Epilogue: Making Mountains out of Molehills 185

Timeline 188

References 191

Select Bibliography 207

Associations and Websites 208

Acknowledgements 209

Photo Acknowledgements 210

Index 211

Foreword

Despite living lives as vibrant as those of any creature, moles receive little of the attention bestowed upon so many others. They remain mysterious, denizens of mazing ecosystems tunnelled out beneath our feet. Moles are mythologized as being unwanted suitors, portrayed as affable personalities in cartoons, even memorialized in a number of poems about death – and yet they are also detested when their hills appear in gardens and fields. The mix of human values projected onto the mole puts the animal in a difficult spot. On the one hand, they are often depicted as sensitive and shy; on the other, many people will not hesitate to eradicate them from their gardens.

Some of the earliest mentions of moles in history come down to us through Greece via religion and philosophy. In the Old Testament, we find them named in Isaiah's prophecy of the day of the Lord: 'In that day people will throw away to the moles and bats their idols of silver and idols of gold, which they made to worship.' (2:20) When Isaiah was translated into Greek, the translators looked at the original Hebrew word, which means 'the burrowers', and used the word ἀσφάλαξ, their word for the mole. Thus moles were negatively lumped in with bats, creatures of the night fit to receive the discarded idols of false gods.[1] Four centuries earlier the Greek philosopher Aristotle, in his landmark work *Metaphysics*, invoked the creature when explaining the idea

Molehill at Stonehenge, January 2019.

7

of 'privation': 'a blind man is not "deprived" of sight in the same sense that a mole is; the latter is "deprived" in virtue of its genus, but the former in virtue of himself.'[2] People, in other words, can help being metaphorically blind, but moles cannot help their literal blindness thanks to nature. We find in Aristotle, quite unintentionally, the very first glimmer of sympathy for moles.

Alongside blindness and horticultural annoyance, moles catch a unique projection of human values: industriousness, wealth, antisocial behaviours, insecurity, anxiety, duplicity, meekness, friendliness and spiritual questing are all seen in representations of the mole. Being creatures of rural areas and suburbs, pastoral connotations also make plenty of sense – moles are not animals of the city. In reality, moles toil, excavating heavy quantities of earth in the dark, at depths where air quality is as poor as it is at high altitudes. Given that their solitary lives of hard work take place out of our sight, the big question about moles – how is it they came to live underground? – has no answer. The space between that mystery and their close proximity to people in many parts of the world encourages an ongoing curiosity about moles that, as we shall see, is worthy of our wonder.

1 Evolution

To this day, the story of how moles evolved their curious underground lifestyle eludes understanding. It also shares its beginnings with the origin of the theory of evolution itself. At the dawn of the nineteenth century, William Paley argued that researching the natural world made it possible 'to infer important aspects of God's *nature* and *character* from the works of creation'.[1] In his 1802 book *Natural Theology*, he used the mole as an example of divine design: 'From soils of all kinds the little pioneer comes forth bright and clean. Inhabiting dirt, it is, of all animals, the neatest.'[2] Meditating upon the fact that its distinctive features – its digging paws and tiny eyes – serve it well, Paley asked, 'What was it therefore which brought them together in the mole? That which brought together the barrel, the chain, and the fuse, in a watch: design; and design, in both cases, inferred, from the relation which the parts bear to one another in the prosecution of a common purpose.'[3] As such, the mole found itself brought into the debate between creationism and evolution practically from the beginning of that dispute.

We also find the creature in Charles Darwin's revolutionary 1859 book *On the Origin of Species*. Darwin reckoned that certain features in animals may have been inherited through a combination of natural selection and disuse, positing a law of variation to explain moles' notoriously limited eyesight:

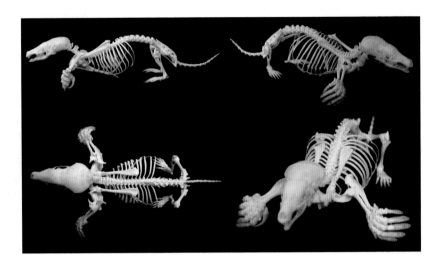

Skeleton of European mole (*Talpa europaea*).

The eyes of moles and some burrowing rodents are rudimentary in size, and in some cases quite covered by skin and fur. This state of the eyes is probably due to gradual reduction from disuse, aided perhaps by natural selection . . . [A] reduction in their size, with the adhesion of the eyelids and growth of fur over them, might in such case be an advantage; and natural selection would aid the effects of disuse.[4]

This notion of inheritance of traits through disuse is not accepted in evolutionary theory today. But again we see the mole used to illustrate a concept that did not stand for long. Darwin struck a more defendable note about moles, however, when using them to explain commonality in difference:

What can be more curious than that the hand of a man, formed for grasping, that of a mole for digging, the leg of a horse, the paddle of the porpoise, and the wing of the bat should all be constructed on the same pattern, and should include similar bones in the same relative positions?[5]

This point, as poetic as it is salient, reminds us of our shared ancestry among mammals. The mole, in the grand scheme of life on Earth, is one of our mammalian associates.

Before the fact of inheritance via chromosomes gained traction, scientists studying evolution were rather limited to the visible evidence. Take, for instance, the work of H. W. Shimer, who inferred evolutionary aspects of moles in 1903 by comparing their anatomy to other species known for digging, such as woodchucks and wombats. His work is typical of evolutionary science before genetics could be studied in fine detail, in focusing on the most obviously peculiar traits – in this case, fossorial adaptations. Fossorial is an adjective meaning burrowing, and it comes up

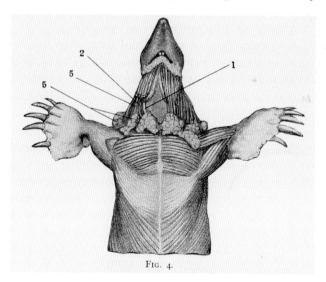

Fig. 4.

Detail of mole's salivary glands, 1913.

again and again throughout formal writings about moles. In the mole's shape and size, Shimer saw a form that logically fitted the demands of life underground: 'small size . . . moderately sized claws . . . face pointed elongate, dentition adapted to food found in the earth'.[6] He erred when claiming moles of the genus *Talpa* possess vestigial, sightless eyes – scientists now know that their eyes, though small, are almost always functional. But the work he did describing how mole anatomy corresponds to a fossorial lifestyle competently laid the groundwork for those who would eventually try to explain how moles evolved. At present, late Eocene fossil specimens from the Isle of Wight and the Hampshire Basin make *Eotalpa* the oldest known talpid mole in the world, dating to 37 million years ago.[7]

Through phylogeny, the study of organisms' evolutionary history, scientists have organized the ancestry of forty living talpid mole species. The designated family Talpidae groups together moles believed to have evolved from a common ancestor, and includes those found across Europe and Asia (Old World moles), North America (New World moles), the shrew moles and desmans. In the past they were taxonomically lumped in with other small insectivores, such as shrews and hedgehogs, but opinions about which species are closely related and which are not have changed. In 2000, Howard P. Whidden conducted a study of mole musculature to try and work out the evolutionary relationship between all species of talpid moles. His findings strengthened the idea of an origin shared by the so-called Old World and New World moles. The shared ancestry 'of the fossorial moles', Whidden found, 'implies at least one dispersal event between Eurasia and North America.'[8] The thinking was that New World moles descended from Old World moles, who had already adapted to life underground. Some scientists still favour this interpretation of data, but the full story is far from told.

INSECTIVORA.

1

Erinaceus europaeus.__ Common Hedgehog.

2

Talpa europæa. Common Mole.

The European mole was long thought to be a close relative of the hedgehog.

There are nine known mole species of the genus *Talpa* in Europe and western Asia. Seeking an updated explanation for their evolution, scientists have estimated that a divergence from eastern species living in Asia occurred during dramatic climatic change in the Miocene–Pliocene. Moles spread rapidly across Eurasia and North America at the time when central Europe peaked in heat and humidity, some 18–16.5 million years ago.[9] They hypothesize that the sudden drop in annual temperature between 14.8 and 13.5 million years ago 'could have also forced

Detail of a common
mole's skull by
Richard Owens,
1866.

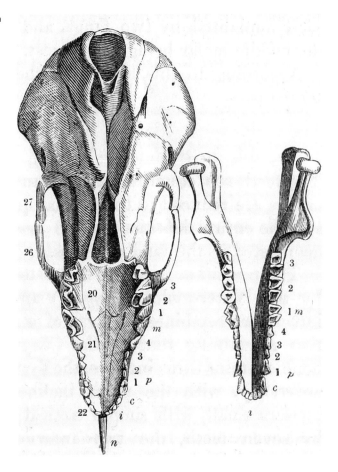

most of the talpids to migrate eastward'.[10] Their understanding
is that the basal split between Old World moles in Europe and
Asia occurred 6 million years ago.

There are currently eight known species of the subfamily
Scalopinae in North America, the New World moles. The oldest

known talpid on the continent is *Oreotalpa florissantensis*, whose teeth and partial jaw were recovered at Florissant Fossil Beds National Monument in Colorado. Before its discovery in 2003, the earliest talpid fossil in North America was dated to the Oligocene (28 million years ago), but *Oreotalpa* pitches that presence back another 6 million years to the late Eocene (34 million years ago). This could make it a contemporary of *Eotalpa*, the oldest known talpid. Karen Lloyd and Jaelyn Eberle lamented having fragmentary evidence but noted it was enough to prove 'talpids had dispersed between North America and Eurasia by late Eocene time.'[11] This opens the dim possibility of a North American origin for moles when Eurasian beginnings have long been favoured. Until more fossils are found, it is difficult to pinpoint exactly where ancestral moles originated.

Talpid moles are not limited to Europe and North America. They are also found throughout Central, East and Southeast Asia, as well as islands like Taiwan and the archipelago of Japan. This is particularly intriguing when we consider that moles are ubiquitous in Britain but cannot be found at all in Ireland. The depth and persistence of the Irish Sea throughout the ages kept moles – and, famously, snakes – out of Ireland. Scientists believe ancestors of as many as nineteen mole species split from European talpids and evolved in the Himalayas and southwestern China before dispersing further east and southeast. Genetic research by Akio Shinohara has found that Central Asia 'was the cradle of multiple dispersion events. Conversely, peripheral parts of the continent, especially the nearby island chains, helped to preserve these distinct mole lineages over time.'[12] Just as moles spread into the Iberian, Italian and Balkan peninsulas, specializing individually in each, they did the same on the Malay Peninsula. A 2005 study of the Malaysian mole's chromosomes found its closest genetic relative is the Japanese mountain mole.[13] Despite vast geographical distance, this surprising finding tells a story of both species descending from the same dispersal out of Central Asia and finding homes in remarkably different directions.

Especially in Japan, moles thrived in isolation from the mainland. The archipelago is home to no fewer than six species of moles (as well as mole-shrews), a rather astonishing variety when considering Britain claims only one. Analysis of DNA suggests four separate migrations of four lineages from continental Asia to Japan.[14] Geological evidence supports this hypothesis. Lower sea levels in the Korean Strait 5.6, 3.5, 2.4 and 1.3 million years ago could have given moles land routes into Japan. Genetic markers indicating divergence in four species of Japanese moles correspond with these dates, 'establishing the Japanese Islands as a hot spot of mole diversity'.[15] The six species living across Japan occupy a range of habitats, from plains to mountain highlands. Those living in areas with friable soil are larger, while those living in tight valleys and on little islands are smaller. One species, known alternatively as the Senkaku mole and the Ryukyu mole, 'is severely under the risk of extinction'.[16] Found only on the tiny isle of Uotsuri-jima in the Senkaku Islands, whose sovereignty is disputed between China, Taiwan and Japan, this mole species is struggling because its ecosystem was damaged by goats introduced in 1978. Today international relations and more than three hundred goats stand in the way of conservation, critically threatening the livelihood of these rare moles.

For all that, some scientists have controversially posited a semi-aquatic origin for moles. Comparing four fossil specimens of extinct moles from Germany with those of living species, scientists point out that old theories about the family having an aquatic origin have recently been backed up by studying moles' myoglobin, a protein found in muscle tissue. Aquatic beginnings with paddle-like paws 'could explain the unusual tunneling

Etching of a European mole with fur (top) and skinned by Georges-Louis Leclerc, comte de Buffon, 18th century.

Fig. 1.

Fig. 2.

Buvee. del.

C.F.Fritzsch. fc.

LA TAUPE
Depouillée de sa Peau.

technique seen in the Talpidae, as well as constraining the two highly fossorial tribes to adapt to a fully subterranean life in the same way'.[17] Strange as it may seem, moles may be built like swimmers because they evolved from swimmers. At least in the case of the star-nosed mole, if they were not swimmers before, at some point they certainly took to the water.

The marsh-dwelling, star-nosed mole's idiosyncratic nose is not mere decoration: its tendrils are covered in sensory organs the likes of which are unseen in any other animal. Scientists call these clusters of nerves Eimer's organs, sensory organs that are found on the snouts of many Old World and New World moles, though never to this extent. As such, they are an intense amplification of an adaptation found in other moles – and they are astonishingly sensitive. Kenneth Catania explains,

> There are 25,000 tiny 'touch domes' on the star, and there
> are 100,000 nerve fibers supplying them . . . To give you a

Star-nosed mole.

good comparison, a human hand, which we know is a very sensitive thing, has about 17,000 touch fibers. The star is only the size of your fingertip. So, imagine five times the acuity and sensitivity of your hand compressed to the size of one fingertip.[18]

This exponential advantage in sensitivity gives the star-nosed mole an almost visual sense of touch, by which it can differentiate between edible prey and specks of grit in fractions of a second.

The star-nosed mole is classified as *Condylura cristata*, the only mole in both its own genus and tribe (*Condylurini*) under the New World subfamily of moles (Scalopinae). Not only is the fossil record patchy with regard to *C. cristata*, its most distinctive feature is made entirely of soft tissue and would not fossilize. It is possible that its predecessors possessed intermediate tendrils – somewhere between those lying flat in the snout and strips arcing off the end of it – but we are unlikely to ever find out for certain. Catania points to the adult coast mole of the American Pacific Northwest for a living example of a mole that, while not ancestral to the star-nosed mole, does possess Eimer's organs embedded in its snout. The Eimer's organs of other moles typically show wear and tear, but the star-nosed mole's do not. Catania suggests the damp, humid, often muddy environment it inhabits is not as hard on its skin, allowing the delicate flesh to flourish in its eccentric way. He also points to the tiny size of its prey as a factor in their evolution: 'Thus, a shift to the wetland environment may have provided both a selective advantage for a more elaborate sensory structure, and the release of a constraint (less abrasive soil) that allowed this structure to evolve.'[19] In any case, the star-nosed mole is without a doubt the most astonishing mole in all of the talpid lineage.

Complicating the view of mole evolution are the golden moles of sub-Saharan Africa and the marsupial moles of Australia. Both are unrelated to the moles covered thus far; they are also unrelated to each other. Neither is a true mole but they have earned the name on the basis of their fossorial lifestyles and features. Evolutionary biologists call this similarity among unrelated species 'convergent evolution', for while all three of these types of moles do not share a recent ancestor, their forms and habits have converged as a result of evolving to similar demands in different parts of the world.

The majority of golden moles, named for their lustrous yellow hair, are found living across the southern tip of Africa. Before genetics could be closely analysed, morphology revealed that these moles were significantly different from others. 'A comparison of the shoulder anatomy of *Chrysochloris* with that of the true moles', Berry Campbell found in 1938, 'shows that the locomotion of the two groups is fundamentally different.'[20] This difference in structure convinced scientists that, while looking and living similarly

Siberian mole (*Talpa altaica*), 18th century.

1

2

1 La grande Taupe du Cap. 2 La Taupe de Canada.

fillement file aqua.

Drawings of the cape mole and star-nosed mole by Georges-Louis Leclerc, comte de Buffon, 18th century.

Skeleton of golden mole (*Chrysochloris trevelyani*) at Dublin's 'Dead Zoo'.

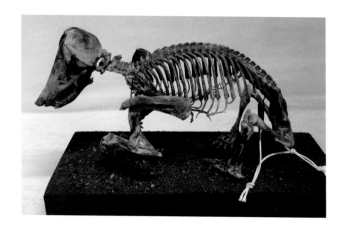

to moles, they were not at all closely related. Genetic analysis in 1998 caused scientists to recommend that golden moles be moved to a new order, Afrosoricida, and that golden moles, along with tenrecs, be moved from Insectivora into it. They estimated that Afrosoricida's common ancestor lived about 70 million years ago 'and that the split between tenrecs and golden moles occurred between 50 and 57 million years age'.[21] If accurate, the ancestor of the golden mole split away from the ancestor of all other moles in the Cretaceous, near the end of the dinosaurs' reign.

To date, there are 21 recognized species of golden mole. This diversity is rather astonishing, given that there are about forty known species of true moles living across Asia, Europe and North America. Golden moles live in sand or sandy soil, a marked distinction from those moles making their homes in loam. This difference of environment has led to unique adaptations, such as seismic sensitivity. Matthew J. Mason and Peter M. Narins note that sound travels better through sand than it does through dense soil: 'This might help to explain the apparent use of seismic sensitivity in prey localization by the desert-dwelling golden mole

Eremitalpa, although the physiological mechanism underlying localization by this animal is unknown.'[22] How these evolutionary adaptations occurred is equally mysterious.

The marsupial moles of Australia, which rather closely resemble the golden mole and make their home in the desert, became mole-like through their own unique evolutionary history. At present there are only two recognized species in one genus, *Notoryctes*. As Michael Archer points out, 'Notoryctids have been used as text-book examples of convergence between themselves and the phylogenetically unrelated but morphologically very similar placental golden moles.'[23] Scientific study of the marsupial mole is exceedingly sparse, given the creature's rarity and the lack of opportunities to research it, but the indigenous Yankunytjatjara and Pitjantjatjara peoples of central Australia have long known of the mole. They call the southern species the *itjaritjari* and the northern one *kakarratul*.

Many of the marsupial mole's features are peculiar. For instance, it has eyes but they are not functional. Analysing the animal's genes, scientists believe the marsupial mole's blindness

Southern marsupial mole (*Notoryctes typhlops*), 1896.

is an effect of disuse reinforced through natural selection, asserting 'phenotypic degeneration of the eyes may be accompanied by parallel changes at the molecular level.'[24] In other words, the blindness occurred in conjunction with mutations in the genome over time. Comparing the middle ear of the marsupial mole with that of the golden mole, scientists were surprised, when expecting similarity, to find difference. Where the golden mole's hearing seems to give it an edge in seismic sensitivity, the structure of the marsupial mole's middle ear shows no signs of this adaptation: 'What is apparent from the comparison of *Notoryctes* and *Eremitalpa* is that similar ecologies do not necessarily give rise to homologous sensory adaptations.'[25] This point is all the more intriguing given later findings about the marsupial mole's ancestral ecology.

In 2011, Archer's team set the record straight on the marsupial mole's evolution, with surprising data. Like moles on other continents, this mole's fossorial ancestor appears to have evolved in the Miocene (22 million years ago). Scientists have long been puzzled by its ancestry since Australia did not have the deserts marsupial moles favour today during the epoch in which its ancestors descended underground. Studying deposits where fossils

Skeleton of southern marsupial mole at Dublin's 'Dead Zoo'.

have been found, Archer inferred that 'despite being confined today to Australia's sandy deserts . . . [marsupial moles] may actually have evolved burrowing adaptations in soft rainforest floors.'[26] Many creatures and plant life are susceptible to extinction if climate changes too drastically, but the marsupial mole teaches us this need not always be the case. How does an animal that evolved in a wet forest adapt to life in an arid desert without seeming to change very much? The transition in environment may not have been so harsh if what worked in moss wound up working in sand, too. Archer's team frames the marsupial mole's rainforest traits as having quite luckily pre-adapted them to the radically different conditions their modern descendants face.

2 Nature

One thing everybody seems to know about moles is that they live in the earth beneath our feet. Subterranean living is the animal's most identifiable characteristic, followed perhaps by its presumed blindness. Despite having such small eyes, most Old World and New World moles can in fact see. A notable exception is the blind mole (*Talpa caeca*), native to Italy and the Balkan peninsula, whose eyes are covered over by skin.

Many people will never have the pleasure of seeing a mole face-to-face. The very first mole I saw was on a country lane in Lancashire, England – and was perfectly flattened. The second mole I saw was in the middle of a hiking trail in Germany's Black Forest and the third was a Townsend's mole on Blanton Ridge in Eugene, Oregon. They, too, had perished. But the number of times I have seen conspicuous evidence of their presence – molehills – is too high to count. As beavers build dams, moles dig tunnels. They are one of nature's mammals that we tend to view as being industrious. Plenty of other animals are known to dig burrows; for instance, badgers, foxes and rabbits all displace earth when setting up a den or warren. Those animals do not, however, cloister themselves in their dugouts. Moles, for the most part, do. Just 11 to 16 centimetres (4 to 6 in.) in length from snout to tail,[1] they can live just out of sight in our midst, making their tunnelled habitat a good place to start when trying to better understand them.

The common mole on Gillies Hill in Cambusbarron, Scotland.

Experts call the tunnels moles dig 'runs' and they are dug at depths ranging from 5 centimetres (2 in.) below the surface to 1.5 metres (5 ft) underground.[2] Moles are not so much soil compactors as they are soil excavators. All dirt clawed out by their strong forepaws must be removed, inevitably leading them to the surface when scooping out space for themselves below. As such, molehills mark those places along a mole's network of tunnels where the detritus of their labour simply had nowhere else to go, akin to piles of earth and rubble people make at worksites when digging a foundation for a new building. Indeed, the bias of comparing moles to the building industry is present in researchers' descriptions of their practices. Gorman and Stone liken the mole's angled sweeps when digging to 'the offset blade of a bulldozer', and Atkinson describes one mole as a 'workaholic' in her endurance when digging.[3] Studying the British mole, he 'calculated that each territory contained a minimum of 1,130 metres [1,236 yd] of tunnel'.[4] If laid end-to-end, this would stretch approximately ten times the length of a football pitch or American football field.

Molehills in Heswall, England.

The mole's paw has an extra digit, a flap that acts as a 'second thumb' in moving soil.

Tunnels can branch and typically are dug to different depths so a mole has access to different soil levels. In dry times, moles will dig deeper underground where there is still some moisture in the soil – insects follow water downward and, if they are to live, moles will follow. Their tunnels can also move through plots of earth already claimed by other moles. Scientists have discovered that, true to their solitary nature, moles deliberately dig tunnels that curve around those of their neighbours. Care is shown towards their tunnels never intersecting, thus maintaining and respecting an innate inclination for privacy. Vicious fights are known to occur between moles when encountering one another.

Moles tend to be active and take rest in four-hour intervals throughout the day. They excavate in tunnels where the air is low in oxygen and high in carbon dioxide, not a great environment for exertion. But they also 'contain twice as much blood and twice as much of the red pigment haemoglobin as other mammals of similar size', giving them the same advantage that high-altitude

Molehills in
fresh snow.

animals like llamas have in breathing thin air.[5] Needing regular places to sleep, they will construct anywhere from one to five nests in their territory. Typically a round chamber, the nest is lined with leaves, grass, scraps of newspaper and even discarded crisp packets. They will also make a toilet of a smaller chamber nearby. In Japan, two species of mushroom are known to grow from the lavatories in mole nests. Thriving from nitrogen in moles' bodily waste, these mushrooms spring up at the ground's surface, which has aided scientists in their work: 'The latrines of moles of genus *Mogera* are usually made near their nests, so that we can find the nests under the fruit bodies.'[6] Since moles do not hibernate, patrolling and digging new tunnels year-round, a dry, insulated space is necessary for survival. Here, where the air is still and comfortable, a European mole can spend as much as half of his or her life asleep.

A curious feature of mole building is an earthen structure commonly referred to as the fortress. These look like mammoth molehills and can even grow over in grass, but they are not just discarded soil. They were once believed to be the mole's equivalent to the beaver's dam, though their construction is uncommon, weakening the comparison. Even in regions where they are known to occur, 'at most one in twenty moles makes them.'[7] When they are built, it is often in areas given to flooding or where the surface soil is not deep enough to support deep tunnels. In building a sizable mound, a mole is able to insulate a proper nest and even construct other chambers, such as a sump for water and a larder for storing stunned earthworms. A fortress can measure over a metre (39 in.) across and one-third of a metre (13 in.) tall, giving a mole plenty of room below to make itself cosy. It might serve as a sort of home base for those moles living in precarious places or those where food is plentiful and mound construction is worth their while. There is no uniform pattern when it comes to the way that fortresses are honeycombed with tunnels and galleries. 'The number and configuration of these varies very much,' Gillian Godfrey and Peter Crowcroft observed, 'and they are not always directly connected with the nest chamber.'[8] No one is sure what inspires moles to put forth the effort in putting one together.

The fortress, 1911.

An alternate
conception of the
fortress, late 1800s.

Fortresses are exceedingly rare, in any case, and remain mysterious to those probing the motivations behind mole behaviour.

Most moles, who moult each spring and autumn, have a coat
that is coloured a dusky grey to slate black. Some moles, however,
have fur that is creamy beige or variant in hue. Though significantly lighter than others, these moles are not albinos. Albino
moles, whose fur is white from a genetic mutation preventing the
production of melanin, do exist, though they are exceedingly

rare. As with many albinos, historically their difference inspired superstition: 'A long held suspicion said that if a mole catcher caught an albino mole, the mole would foretell his own death.'[9] Lighter-coloured moles, cream or reddish, are a bit more common and owe their patchy coats to leucism, a genetic condition affecting pigmentation. Still other moles may have sections of reddish and orange fur, which are attributed to erythrism, yet another congenital condition. The range of coloration in moles may relate to the fact that their appearance has little to do with mate selection, which happens with poor eyesight in the dark. The prevalence of darker moles may also relate to the trouble that faces leucistic moles when they make forays above ground in search of a new home as fledglings. Predators are more likely to spot and eat a pale-coloured mole, even at night, than they are one who can blend in with the dark. If dark moles fare better in evading the gaze of owls and foxes when establishing their territories or embarking on mating rounds, it follows that they will have higher chances of bearing and siring young than their leucistic brothers and sisters.

Moles are insectivores, so their diet varies from place to place, depending on what bugs and invertebrates are around.

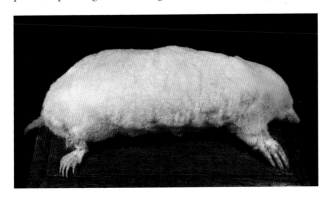

Albino mole.

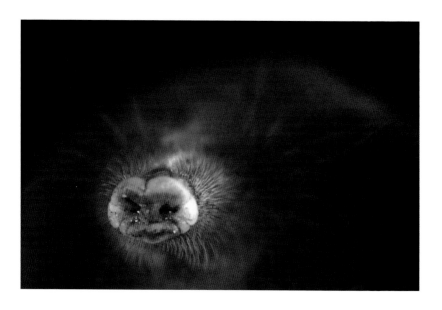

The mole's nose is sensitive and covered in vibrissae.

With this in mind, the earthworm is, more often than not, the staple. Researchers have noted with some pleasure the particular way in which moles go about eating a worm, perhaps because it shows a culinary preference that is altogether relatable. A worm eating its way through the earth will carry along its digestive tract a long line of mud. Bite into an unprepared worm and you will taste the grit of clay, fouling an otherwise reliable source of protein and fat. Moles' mouths are much smaller than ours, making the prospect of a mouthful of worm all the more troubling. In response to this conundrum, moles will grab a worm head-first and draw it tightly through their forepaws while they down it like a strand of spaghetti, forcing the digested soil through its backside. Y.-H. Imaizumi published his own studies on methods moles use when hunting earthworms, discovering two primary techniques employed by the small Japanese mole, the species he named for himself (*Mogera imaizumii*): 'back-with-grip', whereby the mole bites a worm and backs up to pull it out of the tunnel wall, and 'bite-and-retreat', which involves repeated bites as the worm struggles, to immobilize it. Furthermore, he noted how moles frequently eat prey from head to tail, thus enjoying an unspoiled meal.[10] Cleaning out their dinner like this, they also do their dentition a favour, as chewing soil wears their teeth down.

Moles will even store stunned worms in special chambers located in their tunnels, which researchers call larders. In order to survive, a mole needs to eat about six decent-sized worms a day. So what happens if a mole finds more worms in its lair than it really needs on any given day? The thrifty creature will give the overstock a bite on the head and deposit it in a storage chamber. Paralysed, the worm joins others being kept for meals on otherwise wormless days. Atkinson notes that one such larder, discovered in Switzerland, contained about two hundred earth-worms, enough food to 'last a mole for at least a month'.[11] He also notes, regarding the stunning of worms, that 'whether [moles]

The European mole up close.

secrete venomous saliva is currently not known.'[12] Apparently, the worms can recover from this trauma and eventually escape if their captor does not get around to eating them in good time. Moles, however, detect subtle vibrations in their tunnels, many species possessing hairs on their tails that are as sensitive as whiskers. Any invertebrate wandering into – or out of – their territory is likely to be devoured.

One idiosyncratic fact about moles is that it can be rather tricky for people to determine whether they are male or female. The external sex organs are nearly identical, the female's clitoris being enlarged to penile dimensions. This ambiguity is internal as well; female European moles have ovotestes in place of ovaries. That is, their reproductive organs produce eggs *and* testosterone. If this seems like a biological contradiction, human assumptions are to blame. Moles' reproductive and hormonal lives are completely natural. Come breeding season, the female's ovaries

Mole photographed above ground, 1911.

36

A rare above-ground sighting of the eastern mole (*Scalopus aquaticus*).

awaken and a small slit between her urinary papilla and anus perforates. This membrane makes penetration possible and 'after mating it closes up, leaving a small scar.'[13]

For moles themselves, of course, there is likely little or no confusion on this point of sexing each other, as the concern only arises when it is time to breed. By early spring, males have so much testosterone pumping through their bodies that, testes swollen, they are compelled to leave their underground life in search of mates. Travelling over the surface, and typically at night, males are probably drawn to the entrance of a female's tunnel by the scent of her urine. Moles apparently urinate often as they go about their business at home; Gorman and Stone describe a female's tunnel as being 'anointed' by her urine, which carries hormonal scent markers that would tell a male the sex of its inhabitant.[14]

Little is known about what happens when moles court. Males have been tracked via radio tag entering females' tunnel systems, staying about an hour, and then leaving, presumably in search of another female. What transpires in that hour? We can only wonder whether a male is received favourably or taken as an intruder. Given moles' extremely solitary lifestyle, it is not a stretch to consider that a male may not be at all welcome in a female's nest. Of course, she may be as buzzing with hormones as he is and more than ready to see him. One molecatcher with seventy years of experience once claimed he saw moles mating above ground on three occasions and found nothing surprising about it.[15] Mate selection, a topic studied by evolutionary biologists, is regarded as typically falling under the responsibility of females in most species of mammals. Does that hold true for talpid moles? If so, how many males will call upon a female to mate? And how does she express her agency when it comes to choosing or rejecting one or several of them? At this point so many answers we could foist upon the mysteries of mole sexuality are purely speculative. Until research is conducted we are left to wonder. All researchers are certain of is that 'it is unusual to find females who are neither pregnant nor lactating in the summer months.'[16] On occasion, a second litter is known to be born in late summer or early autumn.

Males have nothing whatsoever to do with the rearing of young, that responsibility falling solely to the mother mole. Two to eight babies will be born hairless, the mean number hovering between three and five for most species. Mothers have four teats, and milk so rich that three weeks after birth, when eyes open for the first time, the young have grown to seventeen times their birth weight.[17] There are suggestions that the young are taught how to hunt in tunnels by their mother, though this has yet to be proven. By seven weeks, young moles are already feeding exclusively on prey caught by themselves. Sometime between two and three months old, they strike off alone.[18] Cresting the ground's surface, they disperse in search of unclaimed territories. If lucky, they will find a stretch of virgin, friable soil or the entrance of an abandoned tunnel system dug by predecessor moles who-knows-when. The dangers are great, given the fledglings' lack of experience and vulnerability to night predators; mole bones are common finds when dissecting pellets regurgitated by owls. Should a mole make it to safety underground once again, he or she can be expected to live for about three years, though one European mole on record was found to be 'a veritable patriarch' at seven years old.[19]

Perhaps the most astonishing member of the extended talpid family is the star-nosed mole. It is native to northeastern North America and stands out for the pink sunburst of fleshy feelers radiating from the end of its snout. Twenty-two rays of varying lengths ring the nostrils, reminiscent of beams of light shining out of a star – hence the creature's popular name. Indeed they give the creature a look that is practically mythological, with scientists

Nestling moles, 1911.

Martyn Gorman and R. David Stone calling them a 'hydra' and 'a Medusa-like rosette'.[20] But these idiosyncratic appendages are more than a bouquet on the tip of this mole's nose; they are highly specialized nerve receptors which give it a sense we humans lack, that of electroreception. Scientists have named the nerves covering these tendrils Eimer's organs, for they are so densely packed in an efficient, honeycomb hexagonal pattern, that with 29,000 receptor sites they can produce for the nearly sightless mole a high-resolution sense of everything they touch. Should something nearby cause a vibration, these specialized nerves catch 'sensory shadows' of whatever is moving.[21] As such, they can likely pick up the tremor of a worm coasting through nearby loam and, when swimming, subtle movements through the water of prey such as minnows and nymphs.

If you want to imagine what it might be like to have Eimer's organs, try putting yourself in their nose, so to speak, with the following experiment. Place both of your hands, palms outward, at the end of your nose. Fan out your fingers, jazz-hands style. Now shut your eyes, shuffle about on the floor and feel your way around, trying to identify by contact alone everything your

A mole digs for cover.

fingers touch. This seems to be how the star-nosed mole 'sees' its environment, be it in lightless tunnels or underwater. Its fleshy tendrils, however, are far more sensitive than our fingers, able to differentiate inedible muck from nutritious larvae by touch alone. Their nostrils, furthermore, are capable of smelling in stereo. Surprisingly, all of this translates into swiftness in eating, the species holding the Guinness World Record for fastest eater among mammals: 'an average "handling time" of 230 milliseconds with the fastest time being 120 milliseconds . . . Comparatively it takes humans 650 milliseconds to respond to red light when driving.'[22] Another way in which the star-nosed mole is rather exceptional: it is semi-aquatic. Skilled in subterranean digging, it also possesses waterproof fur and keen agility when hunting for food underwater. Add to this the fact that its tail swells to four times its original size with fat storage for enduring the cold winter months and the star-nosed mole is unique not only among moles, but in the animal kingdom as a whole.

Star-nosed mole's
forepaws and
claws.

There exist some animals that have been named moles despite
their having no actual relation to Old World and New World
moles; these are the mole rat and the mysterious, communal
naked mole rat. Neither moles nor rats, these creatures are named
by approximation, their lives definitely being fossorial but with
ancestry altogether different from moles. True moles, however,
are not the only members of the family Talpidae. Relatives, for
instance, include the shrew-moles of Asia and the west coast of
North America. There are also the desmans, two exceedingly rare
and ancient mammal species that exist today only in the Pyrenees, the northwest corner of the Iberian peninsula, and the
Volga, Don and Ural river basins in Russia, Ukraine and Kazakh-
stan. Known in Portugal as *toupeira-d'água* (the water mole), it
burrows in riverbanks and leads a semi-aquatic life, hunting for
insects and small fish in rilling, clean, alpine streams with deep
pools. Prehistorically common across all of Europe, including
Britain, it now is to be found only in relict populations living at
either end of the continent.

The desman's unique features cast it as a critter an animator might dream up for a cartoon about an earlier era of mammalian life – especially given its long snout with nostrils opening not below but on top. This rubbery nose is adapted to a life of stream and mud-puddle foraging, working as a flexible, flesh-and-blood snorkel. Embedded with whiskers and Eimer's organs, the snout is also the animal's secret weapon in rooting out larvae from streambeds. A natural swimmer, it comes equipped for the water with webbed hind feet and a long tail that is narrowed vertically like a rudder. Unlike moles, desmans do not appear to be territorial, researchers having observed them sharing resting sites regardless of sex. A radio-tracking study led by Yolanda Melero caused the researchers to 'believe that the species may not have the solitary and aggressive character previously accepted'.[23] From continued work on Pyrenean desmans, they have posited 'a social organization hypothesis in which individuals are neither aggressive nor territorial'.[24] Unfortunately, the territory they inhabit is shrinking at an alarming pace. 'More than two thirds of the stream network of the French Pyrenees has experienced a decrease in species occurrence probability by more than 40%' in the last 25

Drawing of desmans, 19th century.

years.[25] Similarly, scientists studying the Russian desman found a marked decline in numbers between 1938 and 2000, which they attribute to climate change and 'the impact of human activities (land amelioration)'.[26] In 2006, it was reported that 'Russian desman numbers are estimated at just 35,000.'[27] Conservation efforts are underway in Spain and Russia, but as conditions and habitat continue to change, the livelihood of the barely studied, charming little water mole leans closer to extinction.

The desman's distinctive snout.

Namibia, South Africa, Mozambique, Zimbabwe and parts of the Congo, Kenya and Somalia are home to another kind of mole altogether. The golden mole, which is the common name given to 21 distinct species, is so different from true moles that it belongs to its own family: Chrysochloridae (Greek for 'golden yellow-green'). Their brunette-to-blond fur coats have an iridescent shimmer that can shine green, purple and bronze, a curious adaptation for a creature that is blind. Indeed, unlike the talpids, these moles cannot see and have both skin and fur growing over undeveloped eyes that never open. Examining the golden mole's blue-green hairs with a scanning electron microscope, Matthew Shawkey found they 'were flattened into paddle shapes, giving a greater surface area to reflect light. Unusually, the scales on each hair contained alternating light and dark layers. Each layer bent the rays of light just like oil on water.'[28] This fetching sheen is likely an effect of their environmental adaptation to life in deserts and sandy soils; a benefit of the gloss is that grains of sand pass right over their hair as they dig. As such, their fur serves a practical use while also possessing a dazzling visual effect they cannot themselves appreciate.

Most golden moles grow no longer than 9 centimetres (3½ in.) from snout to rear, though the giant golden mole (*Chrysospalax trevelyani*) can be 25 centimetres (10 in.) in length. A major difference from the talpids can be seen in the shape of their forepaws. Golden moles do not sport the same kind of spade-like paws, though theirs are also adapted to digging. Typically two of their toes feature sizable claws by which they move earth in rapid scratching strokes. Their exaggerated claws act like picks, striking the sand to scuttle and burrow through it. Moving sand does not require the muscle necessary for pushing soil heavy with clay, so golden moles make do with daintier paws. Their hind feet are also typically webbed, which helps collect earth and kick it behind them as they dig. Their habit of dipping through sand to squirm through it has also led to them being called 'sand swimmers'. In profile, their head, 'capped with a leathery patch' at the end of their snout, looks like a chisel, another aid in pushing forward through ground.[29]

Golden moles occupy 'habitats ranging from coastal and afro-montane forests to woodland savanna and temperate grasslands'.[30] Those in areas with enough moisture to support underground chambers will tunnel more along the lines of true moles, defending their territory with a strong preference for the solitary life. Some species, such as the Hottentot golden mole, are known to share parts of their tunnel systems with herbivorous mole-rats (*Cryptomys hottentotus*); it is thought they tolerate one another because they are not competing for the same sources of food and benefit from the work of a fellow burrower. Possessing some level of concern for cleanliness, they also tend to fashion at least one toilet chamber. Other differences from true moles include the lack of a tail and both males and females having a cloaca for expelling urinary waste. Their often arid lifestyle calls for highly efficient kidneys that can process and retain moisture. Scientists speculate

Etching of a cape mole (*Chrysochloris asiatica*) by P. Mazell, 19th century.

that because of this, some golden moles may never take a single drink of water in their entire lives.

To our eye, golden moles appear to be exceptionally streamlined, shaped like small, flexible potatoes. Except for the capped-nose and fore-claws, nothing sticks out, not even ears, which are reduced to fur-covered holes. While lacking outer ears, the cochleas of their inner ears are tightly coiled in such a way that they can hear extremely low, even seismic vibrations. The middle ear of the Cape golden mole, for instance, 'has been shown to respond to substrate vibrations and airborne sound' in the laboratory.[31] This means they can pick up the sound of insects walking on the sand or burrowing through it. Hearing the footsteps of small prey compensates for their total lack of sight and it is thought that those living in dunes can navigate towards insect-rich tussocks thanks to the sounds of wind-blown grass reverberating through their roots. As foragers in often arid environments, the ability to locate meals as they come is crucial. Golden moles have been known to feed on earthworms, larvae, crickets, termites, spiders and even small lizards.

Golden moles are solitary but will typically come together to mate in the spring. Males and females find each other by squeaking and chirping out calls and, perhaps to locate each other more precisely, males will stamp their feet to signal pursuit. Mating can be a violent experience when a female rejects the potential mate, leading on occasion to death. Females carry one to three young for four to six weeks and rear them alone in a burrow nest made cosier with cut grass. Two or three months later, the young are old enough to fend for themselves and are driven out to make do on their own. Due to the lack of research carried out on golden moles, no one is sure of the animal's average lifespan.

Another curious feature of golden moles is their ability to go into torpor, a physical state similar to hibernation that they can

Golden mole found at Umdoni Park, South Africa.

sustain for about three days. Such a trait is useful for creatures living in environments that experience extreme conditions. By slowing their metabolic rate, they can conserve energy and more or less wait out harsh changes in conditions, 'either daily or in response to cold temperatures'.[32] Even in normal sleep their bodies also cease thermal regulation, dropping their body temperature close to that of the surrounding soil. A variable metabolism allows golden moles to spend their energy wisely, a trait that makes all the difference between life and death in a long dry spell when food is difficult to come by.

Over half of the 21 species of golden mole are currently threatened with extinction. The Endangered Wildlife Trust of South Africa listed five species as endangered in 2016 and one, De Winton's golden mole, as possibly extinct.[33] This is due in large part to habitat loss. The sprawl of human infrastructure and sand mining have cut through – and cut off – populations and decreased their range. Something as simple to us as a paved road can form a boundary that spells isolation for the golden mole. As South African suburbs encroach on their territory, golden moles are finding allies in people working to raise awareness of their plight and drum up conservation efforts so more species will not be lost.

The continent of Australia, famously home to so many distinct marsupial species, is home to two kinds of marsupial moles. The southern marsupial mole (*Notoryctes typhlops*) is known to indigenous peoples as *itjaritjari*; the northern marsupial mole (*Notoryctes caurinus*) is called *kakarratul*. Neither is related to moles found on other continents, though they resemble the golden moles of Africa. Their large forelimbs are good at digging, for instance, though their strokes through soil and sand are made vertically, as opposed to the breast-strokes of common moles. Two of the toes on their front feet are crowned in long, blade-like nails that work to claw through sand. Their nose is covered in a hairless callus that shields their face from abrasion as they dig. Despite that, their sense of smell appears to be quite robust based on the development of their nervous system. There are no ears, merely holes on either side of the head. These moles are also completely blind, as 'only small vestigial buds beneath the surface of the skin remain of the eyes.'[34] Like the golden moles of sub-Saharan Africa, their fur ranges in colour from yellow to cream with a bright sheen. The northern marsupial mole can be coloured pink to cinnamon and the coats of both species can undergo environmental tinting because of the high content of iron oxide in the soil of the outback.

While proficient at digging, the extent of the marsupial mole's habit of backfilling deeper tunnels has yet to be studied. It is known to inhabit dunes, leaving a small furrow on the surface marking its underground path when shallow. The air found between grains of sand is apparently enough for them to breathe, and some scientists credit them with aerating soil in a beneficial way. When seen on the surface, they often scuttle with a slow clumsiness, often going back underground after travelling a metre or so in the sun. They can also lower their metabolism to let their body temperature hover around that of the surrounding sand. Unlike golden moles, they do possess a short tail. Resilient against injury while digging, the 'last five cervical vertebrae are fused, apparently to brace the neck when the animal pushes against the soil with its head'.[35] Nose to tail they can measure from 9 to 18 centimetres (3 to 7 in.). Like other kinds of moles, these animals have an appetite for invertebrates, eating the larvae and pupae of ants, termites, sawflies, beetles and cossid moths. They also are known to eat small reptiles and salamanders, alongside the seeds of plants, making their palate a bit broader than that of most moles. Scientists suspect they play a useful role in keeping pest insect levels in check. The shape of their forepaws, sporting two massive claws each, makes handling food tricky and precludes them from consuming larger prey. In turn, they occasionally become meals for introduced predators such as red foxes and dingoes.

Encounters with humans are extremely rare. Scientists lament how rare sightings of the southern marsupial mole are nowadays. In the early 1900s, Aboriginal people traded their pelts with Europeans, a few thousand changing hands at a time when moleskin was fashionable. 'Since then, specimens and sightings have averaged 5–10 per decade,' a testament to their elusiveness.[36] The very first specimen known to Western science was discovered basking under a tussock of bunchgrass on Idracowra Pastoral Lease in the Northern Territory in 1888. When the director of the South Australian Museum eventually received its remains later that year in an otherwise empty cartridge box, its pouch had decomposed, which led to its not initially being classified as a marsupial. However, as with all marsupials, these animals possess a pouch in which their infant young are suckled for a time after

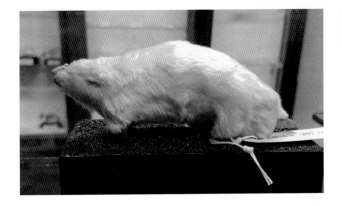

Stuffed southern marsupial mole at Dublin's 'Dead Zoo'.

birth. There are only two teats inside, enough to accommodate two offspring, which are born in November. The pouch opens backwards, a feature that prevents it from collecting sand as they dig forward. Scientists are not sure about their closest ancestral relatives, but some reckon they may share an ancestor with bandicoots, based on their teeth formation. Indeed, much about these animals remains to be learned. There is no evidence available to indicate their average lifespan, how mating occurs or how long young are reared before striking off on their own. Even whether they are nocturnal or active at times throughout the day and night remains a mystery.

Exceedingly little is known about marsupial moles. The Australian government has listed them as endangered, though Joe Benshemesh has suggested this may be an assumption based on a lack of information. He has led expeditions in an effort to map the marsupial mole's range of habitat.

'In very good mole country, such as around Uluru/Ayers Rock and Watarrka National Park, you'll have 70–90 per cent chance of finding tunnels in your trenches,' he says . . .

'It may in fact be one of the most common marsupials in the arid zone.'[37]

Aboriginal peoples have shared that marsupial moles are more likely to be seen above ground after seasonal rains and during windy periods. Hoping to learn more, the Australian Department of Parks and Wildlife encourages anybody encountering one to refrain from handling it but take a picture and then contact them with details of the sighting. Aboriginal Australians are crucial to the study of the marsupial mole being possible in the first place:

> their involvement has been instrumental in virtually every-thing that has been learnt about the species . . . Aboriginal people who still have good tracking skills are able to recognize and interpret subtle signs and tracks, and are often willing to teach these skills to researchers.[38]

Such cooperation could lead towards determining what conservation options are possible to ensure that *itjaritjari* and *kakarratul* continue to live.

3 Scientific Study

Today the endeavour to understand moles within the sciences has become fully interdisciplinary. Scientists in fields like phylogeny, morphology, genetics, palaeontology, molecular biology, osteology and biogeography are trying to do for moles what has been done for the knowledge of so many other mammals. Long neglected by the sciences, moles are just now emerging with complex histories and habits – and the story of how they have been studied from past to present is worth exploring in its own right.

A Latin bestiary from the twelfth century reveals misconceptions about the mole that persist to this day: 'The mole is called Talpa because it is condemned to perpetual blindness in dark places. It is without eyes. It always digs through the ground and carries out the soil, and it gobbles up the roots beneath the fruits, wherefore the Greeks call it "*aphala*".'[1] The idea that moles cannot see is a stereotype of the species; rather than being blind, however, here they are said to lack eyes altogether. Translator T. H. White notes, 'ἄφαλος means "without the boss in which the plume of a helmet is fixed". Perhaps this might apply to a plant with no roots. Or perhaps the reference is to φαλλός, in which case the mole is regarded as emasculating the plants.'[2] Either way, the original author is incorrect altogether, as the European moles in question are devoted insectivores, not devourers of plants.

Mole in bottom
margin of
*Topographia
Hiberniae*
(*c.* 1196–1223).

Moles appear almost four hundred years later in the *Hortus sanitatis* (Garden of Health), the first encyclopaedia of natural history. The 1491 edition, now housed at the University of Cambridge, mentions that moles are blind and born out of the earth, digging in the soil, getting nourishment from worms and the roots of grain. It also makes the rather bold claim that burning a mole to ash, mixing it with egg white and spreading it on one's face can remedy leprosy – or at the very least psoriasis, depending on how one translates the original Latin.[3] One of the most charming aspects of this volume is its woodcut illustrations, likely done by a person who had never actually seen the moles, mermaids or dragons described therein. The woodcut of moles presents a pair looking more like hamsters, their forepaws spindly and not at all mole-like. The artist also completely left out the eyes, visual shorthand for their assumed blindness.

Medieval mole
from the Ashmole
Bestiary,
c. 1201–25.

tuuum for Alij dicunt mr moie ham hrf in crefcr tum turfi defia

Alpa dicta quoo fir da

Medieval mole from an illuminated text.

Conrad Gessner fashioned a woodcut of the mole for his *Icones animalium*, whose editions were published from 1551 to 1587.[4] His representation looks much more like a mole, with its narrow snout, enlarged forelimbs and slight hindlimbs all where they should be. It even has eyes. Along with the cross-hatched likeness, Gessner also provided the words for mole in Latin, Spanish, Italian, French and German. No mole-infused skincare poultices are propounded, but the quality of Gessner's art shows he had clearly encountered moles, perhaps even drawing this one from a specimen before him.

In the eighteenth century, Georges-Louis Leclerc, comte de Buffon, included several likenesses of the mole in the *Histoire naturelle*. The leading naturalist of his day, he published 36 volumes of his natural history series, an exhaustive project that lasted his adult life. The tome's etching of a European mole, posed

before an incongruous backdrop of classical architecture, is still impressive in its realism. The drawing of the North American star-nosed mole, however, is less convincing: it shows the nose's floret but also gives the mole serpentine eyes, no distinctness to the forelimbs, and a tail, drawn longer and rattier than in life, that is incorrectly segmented. Perhaps it was drawn from descriptions or a specimen that had become rather the worse for wear by the time it reached France. One curious criticism of Buffon's work comes from James Madison, fourth president of the United States, in the postscript to a letter written to third president Thomas Jefferson on 12 May 1786. Madison shares variations in the weight and dentition of European and American moles, suggesting the mole is the exception to a contemporary theory that species common to the Old World and New World had merely migrated from one to the other. He adds, with a flair for interior decor, that 'if arranged in frames, [Buffon's engravings] would make both an agreeable & instructive piece of wall furniture.'[5]

In 1829, Étienne François Dralet published a slim book on moles in Paris: *L'Art du taupier, ou Méthode amusante et infaillible de prendre les taupes* (The Art of the Mole-catcher; or, The Fun and Infallible Method of Catching Moles). Dralet's may be the very first book devoted solely to the scientific study of moles, providing readers in France with an understanding of the common European mole's biology, lifestyle and range of habitat. Here its genus and species were recorded as *Taupe woogura*, a name that would

Moles in *Hortus sanitatis* (1491).

Etching of the
European mole
by Georges-Louis
Leclerc, comte
de Buffon,
18th century.

not survive revision as taxonomy became standardized. He also covers the difficulty of keeping moles for research; citing Geoffroy Saint-Hilaire, a contemporaneous scholar, Dralet highlights the dangers of keeping two moles together:

> do not go, believing to procure for moles the satisfaction of companionship, to keep two in an enclosed place without food; this is to deliver the weaker to the tooth of the stronger. In vain one tries to flee, the other showing in its pursuit only more vehemence and fury. The weaker soon expiates her helplessness; she is devoured.[6]

This study, while not up to the rigour of the sciences today, shows considerable knowledge of the species. Present, for instance, is the understanding that European moles are active at peak times throughout the day (Dralet puts it at four times); researchers Gillian Godfrey and Rob Atkinson, working one hundred years later, verified this with tagging and tracking (Atkinson puts it at

LATINE Talpa.   ITALICE Talpa.
HISPANICE Tópo.   GALLICE Taulpe.

GERM. Maulwerff/Moll/Mollmuß/Scherrmuß.

Mole by
Conrad Gessner,
16th century.

58

De Seve del.   B. de Bakker sc.

LA TAUPE.

LA TAUPE DE CANADA.

three times for moles with ample food, noting a more frenetic pattern for those living in precarity).[7]

Dralet reproduces Hilaire's 'very faithful drawing of a survey of ground done in 1825', essentially a map of tunnels and corresponding molehills that measured 24 metres (80 ft) long and 15 metres (50 ft) wide at a location along the river near Pontoise.[8] He also provides 42 'principles' about the mole, imparted as essential knowledge for anyone intent on eradicating them. He presents eight situations one may encounter in the endeavour and how to handle them, complete with illustrations of typical molehill and tunnel patterns. This is followed by descriptions and diagrams of various mole traps devised in France and Bavaria. Dralet's popular volume on pest control, republished and expanded in 1856 and 1880 in France, experienced a robust publication history throughout the nineteenth century.

In the 1950s, an English zoologist named Gillian Godfrey took the first giant leap in fieldwork on the mole, though her practices proved unsafe for moles and scientists alike. Godfrey earned a doctorate at the University of Oxford in 1953, the first woman to do so in the Bureau of Animal Population. She quickly advanced knowledge on the underground movements of moles through the practice of radioactive tracking, an innovation she devised while

Etching of a star-nosed mole by Georges-Louis Leclerc, comte de Buffon, 18th century.

W. Hollar fecit, 1646.

Dead mole by Wenceslaus Hollar, 1646.

previously studying voles. Noting that the European mole's tail is thicker at its end than at its base, she would affix there a small metal ring with a radioactive capsule soldered to it. At the base, it would not slip off, tagging the mole in such a way that it could freely go about its business. By positioning a Geiger counter on the end of a pole, Godfrey was free to track the positions of tagged moles from above ground. Her apparatus could pick up readings so long as a mole did not descend more than 30 cm (1 ft) underground, and thereby she was the first scientist not only to chart out their tunnel systems in detail but to report on their unseen movements throughout the day in their natural habitat. 'There is now ample evidence that moles can be located and followed with a Geiger counter without being alarmed,' Godfrey and her husband Peter Crowcroft observed, 'and at times, in fact, they have been seen to emerge from the ground beside the observer's feet.'[9]

While effective, this method unfortunately relied upon handling radioactive material and exposing moles to it for extended periods of time. Cobalt-60, the substance used, is a synthetic isotope capable of causing illness and cancer. As such, Godfrey and

Gillian Godfrey tracking a mole with a Geiger counter, 1954.

her test subjects were put at risk. She also had to carefully monitor each mole – she used this method on only one mole at a time – lest it venture off and inadvertently expose somebody to gamma radiation. Given modern safety standards and regulations, this experiment would not be conducted today, but her work paved the way for radio-tracking, which is benign to the health of tagged animals and became a norm among zoologists. With Crowcroft, Godfrey published *The Life of the Mole* in 1960. There, in the first book-length study of the mole, she extended her discoveries to the general reader. In the light all of these accomplishments, Godfrey deserves to be remembered not only as the first scientist who substantively expanded our knowledge of how moles live, but as one of the pioneering women in the sciences.

The next major names in the study of moles are Martyn L. Gorman and R. David Stone, who conducted research at the University of Aberdeen in Scotland. Their 1990 book *The Natural History of Moles* brought all the latest methods of collecting and interpreting data to the subject of moles, focusing particularly on the European mole. Their seminal work contains complex equations for determining the force with which moles dig, graphs depicting the economics of digging tunnels and computer simulations charting the impact of trapping on mole populations. Gorman and Stone's book truly marks the maturation of mole research, with comprehensive descriptions of lifestyle habits, diet and an array of illustrations. It even sensationalizes, with what Gorman and Stone call a 'scene of carnage', reproducing a grizzly photo and accompanying X-ray of a gull and mole that had been analysed in the journal *Scottish Birds* in 1972: 'the mole had been swallowed alive and probably undamaged. As it was swallowed it had made a 2 cm tear in the top of the gull's oesophagus . . . The mole then tore through the stomach wall . . . [and] died of suffocation, coupled with exhaustion and shock.'[10] Alongside

John James
Audubon's
painting of
hairy-tailed
moles,
19th century.

such violent titillation, their breadth of knowledge and analysis of data established a solid understanding of how the European mole lives and dies.

Contemporaneous with Gorman and Stone was the work of Rob Atkinson at the University of Oxford. He published his findings for the general reader as a book in 2013, *Moles* – a must-read for anyone wanting to know more about moles, from someone who built his career studying them. His approach to educating the public is charming and his style exceptionally readable. Forgoing dizzying formulae and charts – though he clearly knows his way around both – for a simply informative approach, Atkinson imparts what he learned throughout his career as a zoologist. His accounts of radio-tracking European moles in the English wild are laced with misadventure and humour. Naming the moles he tracked alphabetically, Atkinson dubbed the first seven Araldite, Bostick, Copydex, Dental Acrylic, Evostick, Fish Glue and Gum. 'I fitted them with radio-transmitters made using Araldite,' he writes, 'which was also, I thought at the time, rather a pretty name for the little female I caught early in my research.'[11] From there he ran out of glues, eventually naming other moles Kylie, for Australian singer Kylie Minogue, and Marc, for English singer Marc Almond.[12] The fieldwork these British scientists conducted in the 1980s and 1990s, greatly expanding our knowledge of moles, was clearly done with passion. Never had so much work been done before – indeed, only about 180 scholarly articles had been written on moles between 1980 and 2010.[13]

Mole research in this century has honed in on microscopic aspects of their lives in astonishing detail while plenty of the more pressing facts of their experience continue to elude. For instance, Mary T. Silcox and Mark F. Teaford have taken a close look at mole dentition. Scanning electron micrographs of molars from North American hairy-tailed moles and coast moles show shallow striations in the teeth, linear grooves often travelling in the same direction. Scoring of this nature is not typical in teeth of other small animals, leading them to conclude that 'this pattern seems consistent with a diet that forces teeth to shear against soil while processing food.'[14] Why does soil regularly scratch moles' molars? Probably because it is often present on – and in – their favourite food: earthworms.

Visiting a laboratory at the University of Massachusetts, Amherst, in 2014, the *New York Times* science writer James Gorman found graduate student Yi-Fen Lin studying Eastern moles digging through tubs filled with, of all things, couscous. Scientists have

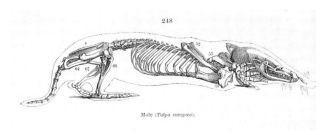

Mole (*Talpa europæa*).

Detail of mole
anatomy, 1866.

long spoken to the difficulties of keeping moles alive in the lab, but Lin defied the naysayers by capturing hairy-tailed moles herself and fulfilling their demanding dietary needs with earthworms, mealworms, eggs and sunflower seeds. Wanting a closer look at their burrowing techniques, she took to X-ray videography of her test subjects ploughing through dry semolina, 'a material chosen for its consistency and uniform particle size'.[15] Those grains show up nicely onscreen, a matrix of trackable pixels. The recordings, in ghostly greyscale, reveal the shoulders, bones and strokes of natural-born swimmers. In 'asking exactly how, and how hard, moles dig', research by Lin and colleagues at Brown University suggests that when it comes to living underground, a semi-aquatic physique serves talpid moles swimmingly.[16] Gorman and Stone record that 'all moles can swim if they have to, albeit slowly and with little style,' covering more than a kilometre (0.9 mi.) in thirty to fifty minutes.[17]

Swimming brings us back to the star-nosed mole, certainly one of the strangest animals in the world. Native to the northeastern wetlands of North America, the species is unabashedly semi-aquatic, digging tunnels through swampy soil and hunting prey in pools of water. These habits are idiosyncratic in their own right, but the real evolutionary mystery of this species is plainly visible on the tip of its nose. A total of 22 fleshy tendrils radiate on all sides of both nostrils, looking as if a cartoon trick cigar exploded at the end of its snout. Their starburst pattern is what inspired its common name.

Research of the star-nosed mole's nervous system from snout to brain carries opportunities to assess our own nervous system and those of other animals. As expected, the unique adaptation has corresponding features in the brain that are just as unusual. The rays around the nostrils are connected to the brain in a way that parallels visual systems in other mammals. As a result,

there also appears to be an added area to the brain cortex that is altogether unique. 'Star-nosed moles conveniently show principles of mammalian brain organization owing to the multiple anatomically visible maps of the star in the neocortex,' Kenneth Catania explains. 'However, they also provide clues to more general biological principles such as theories of predator diet selection or the relationship between development and evolution.'[18] For instance, the star-nosed mole's nose validates optimal foraging theory, whereby species have specialized in ways that lessen their energy output when obtaining and eating food. Indeed, 'star-nosed moles have the shortest handling time documented for any mammal when consuming small prey.'[19] This species is sure to render more revelations as research into its habits and make-up continues.

Baby star-nosed moles, 2013.

Running parallel to research in Europe and North America, the scientific study of moles in East Asia, and particularly Japan, has its own heroes who have committed their lives to the field since the mid-twentieth century. Given Japan's diversity with six native mole species, there is much to be discovered. The first big name in Japanese mole science was Yoshiharu Imaizumi, who between 1960 and the 1980s studied everything from moles' hunting habits to the subtle differentiations between species.

Zoologist Shin-ichiro Kawada dissecting a mole.

Alexei Abramov's photo of *Euroscaptor orlovi*, newly discovered in Vietnam and Yunnan, China, 2016.

His work was not published in English, but that of his successors has been, meaning the enthusiastic mole research currently happening in Japan is more accessible than ever. For instance, in 2012, Shin-ichiro Kawada discovered a new species of mole living in the semi-deciduous forests of the Tam Dao foothills in northern Vietnam. It was grouped into the genus *Euroscaptor* and given the species name *subanura*. This mole has unique features, such as bumpy 'protuberances surrounding the nostrils', an 'extremely short tail . . . which visually resembles a wart' and 'armorlike morphology . . . only seen in this species'.[20] Indeed, its ribs are thick, the ribcage packed tightly without the breezy gaps typical in other moles. Work like this reminds us that unknown species may still await discovery and study.

While research on true moles is now taking off, that on golden moles and marsupial moles is still only just beginning. Research into the golden mole, though it was recognized by the great taxonomist Carl Linnaeus 250 years ago, is still in its infancy. In 2017, a featurette on the golden mole broadcast by the South

Study of the
marsupial mole
by Angel Cabrera,
1919.

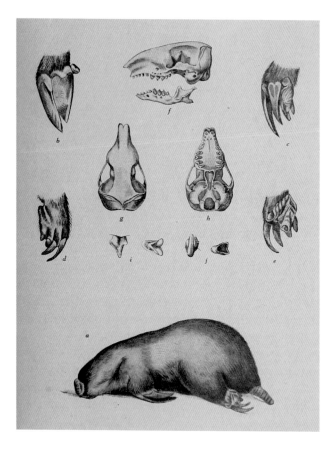

African Broadcasting Corporation encouraged local viewers to provide scientists with any remains that might turn up on their doorsteps: 'If your cat brings in something that looks like a regular mole please double-check. If it doesn't have ears, eyes or a tail, please contact Bradley [Gibbons] at the [Endangered Wildlife Trust] . . . to ensure the enchanting world of these endearing, underground engineers persists.'[21] Specimens contributed by ordinary South Africans could provide great insights into these curious little creatures and improve conservation efforts.

In terms of where the study of marsupial moles goes next, Joe Benshemesh made a discovery about their fossorial habits that should give researchers an edge in finding specimens to examine. Scientists long believed the marsupial mole was a 'sand-swimmer' like the Namibian golden mole, scuttling just under the surface in dry sand without enough structural support for permanent tunnels. But in 2014 Benshemesh found this assumption was wrong: 'Perhaps the most significant finding of this study is also the simplest: the underground tunnels of itjaritjari are clearly detectable underground in the form of backfilled tunnels.'[22] The marsupial mole does in fact create longstanding tunnels and goes so far as to backfill them as it digs. Whereas researchers expected to find the animal just under the ground's surface, the discovery of these passageways directs their attention deeper. 'The distinction between sand swimming and tunneling is important,' Benshemesh observes, 'because the assumption that no signs of itjaritjari exist underground has inhibited research into the distribution, abundance, and conservation status of these unique species that are regarded as endangered.'[23] One of the most important aspects of studying an animal, after all, is knowing where to find it.

4 Moles in Myth and Folklore

Aesop of ancient Greece told the fable of the mole and his mother, in which the little blind mole boasts he can see. His mum, testing his sense of smell, finds him to be not only blind but hard of smelling, too.[1] The moral is that boasting beyond one's abilities will reveal other shortcomings – a curious notion to be mapped onto the mole. Though its poor eyesight is famous, its industriousness and elusive underground nature have led to other kinds of appreciation. French symbologists Jean Chevalier and Alain Gheerbrant explicate its significance as a spiritual guide among early agricultural peoples:

> If ever there was a chthonian animal, it is the mole which symbolizes all of the powers of Earth . . . Moles were regarded as symbols of the person who unfolded the mysteries of Earth and of death which, once acquired, preserved the initiate from sickness or brought a cure. From the physical plane, that of the agrarian cult-animal, the symbol permitted transition to the spiritual plane, that of the master who guides the soul through the gloomy underground maze and heals it of its passions and anxieties.[2]

Moles, as we shall see, outwit tricksters, often appear in stories of marriage proposals gone wrong and are almost always punished – by themselves or the gods – in myths and folk tales the world over.

There has been scholarly debate on the mole's place in another aspect of ancient Greek culture. Ailing believers in Asclepius, god of healing, used to spend nights in his temples, hoping the dreams he brought would cure them of their illnesses. A trio of classicists argued in 1949 that the etymology of the name Asclepius points back to 'the mole-hero'.[3] They supported their reasoning by pointing out that the Tholos in Epidaurus, a small round temple to Asclepius containing a subterranean labyrinth, resembles a mole-hill. Others were not so sure about this mole connection, finding it likelier that Asclepius' name pre-dates the Greek language and crossed into it.[4] One can see why some might connect the burrowing, underworld animal with the god who heals through dreams brought in the deep darkness of sleep. This association could be entirely mistaken – there is ample direct evidence of snakes being associated with the god and kept as sacred inhabitants at his temples – but as a symbol in an early agrarian society,

Samuel Howitt's illustration for Aesop's other mole fable: 'Ass, Ape and Mole', c. 1810.

the mole was seen as existing on a spiritual level as a guide to those who are ailing through the darkness of sickness towards health. Related to this, a comparative connection was drawn between Asclepius and Rudra, the archer-god of healing in Hinduism, whose animal associate is indeed the mole.[5] It has also been argued that snakes tend to overshadow moles in people's imagination, so if snakes did supplant moles in the cult of Asclepius it is understandable why moles were forgotten in this capacity – and besides, the origins of ancient rites are almost all lost anyway.[6]

Being native to North America, moles naturally appear in stories told by indigenous Americans of many cultures across the continent. Naraya, the Shoshone Ghost Dance, understands that the 'mole has power to cause thunder.'[7] Pueblo tribes revere the mole as a medicine animal, being one of their six directional guardians; fittingly, its realm is that of the underworld, where it holds sway over 'the color black, earth and agriculture, and sickness and health'.[8] An Achomawi story about the mole, on the other hand, puts it in celestial contact with the sun and explains the curious positions of its front paws:

Once the Sun fell down from the sky just about sunrise. Mole caught it, and held it up until people got there and helped him to shove it back. The Sun had meant to roll along on the ground instead of in the sky. It was from holding up the Sun the Mole's hands are bent so far back.[9]

In Salish lore, Pul'-laqu-whu – Mole, the Mound Digger – was married to the wily trickster, Coyote: 'Mole was a good woman, always loyal to her husband in spite of his mean ways, his mischief-making, and his foolishness. She never was jealous, never talked back, never replied to his words of abuse.'[10] She found herself compelled to provide for their family while he

Kevin Storrar's illustration of Crime Officer Mole in *Skinned in the Willows* by Steve Gronert Ellerhoff (2016).

loafed, a problem that came to a head when he failed to slay a fawn she had caught and ate all the rose hips she had gathered for the children. The ensuing fight ended with his stabbing at her with his flint blade as she escaped underground. When his knife struck the earth, she marked the point with some *tul-meen* (red facial paint), fooling him into thinking she was dead. He dropped several of his sons at their Uncle Kingfisher's to learn how to hunt and took off with his youngest without a destination in mind. After wandering hungrily for days, they found a woman on the prairie who was digging for roots. She made him nostalgic for his wife and when he asked her for good news, she said, "'Coyote deserted his children and killed his wife!'"[11] Coyote suddenly realized it was his wife, Mole, and moved to kill her with his knife. Once again, she evaded him, disappearing underground. Mole triumphs in escaping her feckless, violent husband, proving herself Coyote's superior in both smarts and commitment to taking care of the family.

In stories of other indigenous North American cultures, the mole is alternatively troublesome and helpful in the lives of people.

75

A Hopi tale tells how Mû'yi (Mole) assists Badger and Coyote in thieving food from the Hopi. On the promise of a substantial cut of the bounty, he digs the tunnel, performs reconnaissance and passes the food down the hole to his cohorts. This is essentially a heist narrative, and his covert approach pays off with enough food to fill his pantry for months.[12] Mole also played the key role as a horse rustler for the Apaches in a story explaining how they came by their steeds. When the Apaches first saw horses and wanted some for themselves, they asked Mole to seize them. He picked out the old mare that led the herd and approached her at the watering hole: 'When she stooped down to drink, Mole made ripples, and these ripples became a rope and got around the mare's neck. Mole had a hold of the other end of the rope and led the mare to a tipi in the village.'[13] Thus the Apaches obtained horses. As such, moles in indigenous American stories have been portrayed as both a nuisance and a boon.

There is also a story of the mole at the time of Christ's crucifixion as told by F. J. of Yaonáhuac, a Nahuat-speaker. The Nahua peoples are indigenous to Mexico and El Salvador. Though Aztec traditions are still observed among the Nahua, they were among those cultures in Central America that were Catholicized through Spanish conquest. As this story goes, the mole paid Christ a special visit when his body had been shut away in the tomb: 'The mole [topo = *tusa*] decided to go into the grave to see if he were alive or dead. God our father was alive. The mole felt that he was alive. God our father said to the mole, "Now that you've come, now you'll stay here forever." So the mole stayed there and didn't return to tell the Jews.'[14] As opposed to other cultures' stories of gods punishing moles, here the mole is allowed to stay in the presence of God, its underground lifestyle being blessed on account of the animal's divine curiosity. Also worth noting is how the story of Easter is creatively built upon by a descendant of a colonized people. Animal lore has long adjoined accounts of the crucifixion in cultures around the globe, providing localized flourishes to a worldwide religion. In this instance, the mole's fossorial ways are explained as a gift from God at the advent of Christ's resurrection.

Hopping continents to Africa, the Bulu of Cameroon tell a story explaining the mole's snout and stink, tying them to his attentiveness in tending a fire when left home alone: 'He blew and blew until his lips lengthened out into a snout. Also the sparks he blew up fell on to his back and singed his hair, covering his body with a bad odor.'[15] Among the Ewe of Togo, Mole is said to play a role in the demise of Spider, a great trickster who, for a time, evades Death. Spider's tactic is to invite an animal for dinner and, when Death comes knocking, send the guest to the door to die. The evening Mole comes for dinner, Spider retires for the night and Mole, missing his own bed, ends up digging a tunnel home. When there is a rap on the door, Spider thinks it must be Mole, answers it and is knocked dead by a log to the head from Death. The story is told 'to teach you that there is more than one clever person in a village'.[16] In this case, that second clever villager is Mole.

The Meru of Kenya also relate the mole to death. According to their tradition, a mole was sent by Murungu, the Supreme God, to deliver the important message to humans that they would be reborn after dying. Unfortunately, the mole was waylaid by a hyena, who was upset by this news: it meant he would no longer be able to dine on people. Bullied into changing the message, the mole told the people that Murungu sent him to say they would die and *never* be reborn. When he returned and told Murungu what had happened, the Supreme God was displeased. 'To punish the mole,' so the story goes, 'Murungu told it that from that time on it would live underground, far from God. That is why the mole lives in a hole in the ground and comes out only at night when no

Congo golden mole (*Calcochloris leucorhinus*) by Joseph Huet, 1885.

one can see it.'[17] This Meru story offers an imaginative explanation for the mole's real-life habits while scapegoating it for the existence of death. The mole is imagined to be timid under pressure, strong-armed by a selfish, cruel hyena. Instead of taking pity on the mole, who was clearly afraid, Murungu banishes it below ground for all its generations. The Kenyan mole species in question, incidentally, is Stuhlmann's golden mole, one of the few species living far north of the continent's southern tip, and yet it bears mythological burdens similar to those ascribed to other kinds of moles in other parts of the world.

There are stories of *itjaritjari* and *kakarratul*, the marsupial moles of Australia, in the traditions of the desert-dwelling Aborigines. Joe Benshemesh and Ken Johnson, who have cooperated with Aboriginal people to study the marsupial mole, note that it has been a figure in their mythology, 'undoubtedly known to [them] for thousands of years'.[18] Aborigines link its presence to places like the Anangu-Pitjantjatjara Lands and trails associated with Dreamtime, their collective cosmology. 'To the Anangu of the Red Centre,' for instance, 'Minyma Itjaritjari is a playful ancestral being who lives in a cave in the side of Uluru.'[19] Ulur is the sandstone monolith known to Westerners as Ayers Rock. Minyma Itjaritjari (which means Marsupial Mole Woman) is said to have been friendly with the *Mala* women – that is, female rufous hare-wallabies – 'and would often come out of her cave to watch the children play'.[20] She also 'built the shelters . . . in the rock [of Uluru] to create a yuu (windbreak). These natural formations were important to the Anangu because they used these caves to teach younger generations as well.'[21] Aboriginal people are known to harbour affection for the 'blind, clumsy, and harmless' marsupial mole, traditionally eating it 'only during hard times' when food proved scarce.[22] These marsupial mole stories and associations are sacred to indigenous people of the outback, and accordingly the moles remain largely protected as cultural and religious knowledge.

The indigenous Ainu of northern Japan, renowned for their rites and beliefs to do with the bear, also tell traditional stories about the mole.[23] Their lore deifies the animal, casting it as an old god who descended to Earth from heaven to become one of the most powerful terrestrial immortals. Indeed, a mole's remains were said to be kept for good luck:

> As then the mole is known to be such a grand and noble deity, his head must be wrapped up in fetich [or 'fetish', meaning magic wood] shavings when he is killed, and reverently kept as a charm. And when he is first killed the men must take the head and worship it, saying, 'O thou divine mole, we know that thou art a great god, henceforth kindly bless us; keep us, and be thou our lord.' If one does this in a reverential manner the mole will bless him and make him very rich.[24]

With that said, his behaviour in the stories is not always benevolent. The Ainu mole god exhibits a range of moods, some of them heroic while others are downright frightening.

One of the most prominent Ainu mole stories falls into the category of matrimonial mole tales. The god of the lower skies decided that his daughter, the most beautiful female ever to have lived, should marry the mole. 'There is no divinity upon earth more honourable and higher in rank than the mole,' he reasoned to her, 'you, my daughter, must wed no other than he.'[25] She consented and the mole was notified, arriving in the heavens for his arranged wedding. The ceremony went to plan and the reception dinner was well underway when the bride slipped out, indicating she would return shortly. She did not. The mole went looking for her then, searching heaven, earth and sea. Acting on a tip, he investigated the grass and there she was, hiding from him:

> He was very angry when he saw her, and, trampling upon her with his feet in a great rage, said, 'O you wretched creature, why did you slip away and hide yourself among the grass? As you have thus disobeyed your father and run away from your home, I will punish you most severely. You may no more return to the heavenly dwellings, but must live in this world only. You shall now be turned into grass.'[26]

The mole trampled his wife with all his strength, the effects of his domestic violence turning her into a plant. Through this abuse, she was renamed *Kunau*, the Ainu word for the flowering crow-foot known in English as Adonis. A disturbing tale, the mole emerges here as possessive, vindictive and ultimately violent – an avatar of toxic masculinity.

In another Ainu story, the mole is shown to have played a central role in the appearance of foxes and cats in the world, all going back to a knock-down, drag-out fight between the mole and a demon named Moshiri-shinnaisam. The ancient demon 'had no beginning, and has always been so evil-disposed that when

God made the world He could not allow him to live in any place where men dwelt'.[27] Despite being so formidable, when Moshiri-shinnaisam challenged him to a contest of strength, 'the mole readily consented, well knowing that an evil demon was no match for a good god.'[28] Their fight began immediately in the mole's home, the demon throwing him into the hearth and burning the mole to ash. When leaving, however, the demon inexplicably found the mole blocking the door. Caught off guard, the mole rolled the demon back to the fire and held him in it. When the demon tried to escape by turning into smoke, 'the mole, divining his intention, blew hard at him so that he at last fell again and again into the fire till he was burned quite up amid much pain and suffering. The ashes alone remained.'[29] Despite having been burned to dust, 'being the remains of a demon, they could not have the life taken out of them. That was impossible. They therefore changed themselves into foxes and cats.'[30] This story of

Mole by Brooklyn artist and animator Jessica Milazzo, 2017.

the mole's unexpected might conveys an explanation for the wily, cunning behaviours perceived in cats and foxes, crediting them with demonic origins.

Foxes and the mole god have a later encounter in Ainu folklore. The story goes that a pair of brother foxes plotted to assume human form and go and cause trouble among men by selling them fraudulent goods made of twigs and leaves. The mole saw them preparing and set about throwing them off, going to the trouble of setting up a facade of an entire human village and disguising himself as an old man in garments made of tree leaves and herbs. He set out meals of mulberries and grapes and invited crows and other birds to people the fake community in human guise. When the foxes arrived in the form of men, they were tricked by the mole's triumph of artifice, delighting in his treasures, the fruit, and the dancing of the villagers. After returning home, the fox brothers decided they should go back to have more of the delicious human food, deciding to barter for it with their homemade treasures. Venturing to the village again, they found it empty, save for a large, golden house. Inside they saw the mole as himself, a 'very venerable god'.[31] Revealing his own trickery, he scolded them for taking human form and peddling counterfeit goods: 'You think this is a human village; but it is the village of me, your master the mole. It seems you constantly do all sorts of bad things. If you do so, it is very wrong; so do not assume human shape anymore. If you will cease to assume human shape, you may henceforth eat your fill of these mulberries and grapes.'[32] Complementing Aesop's famous fable, he suggests that the crows may be able to drop some fruit for them as they please. Foxes in other parts of Japan are still said to take human form,[33] but these foxes agreed to give up the habit, explaining, at least among the Ainu, why foxes and crows can be seen feeding in each other's company. The mole god here is shown to win by outfoxing foxes.

Looking to the rest of Japan, a haiku from 1682 expresses what is perhaps the most confounding view on moles in extant literature:

asahi island
a mole has become
a sea slug

~

asahi island
where a molehill grew
into a sea slug

~

sunrise island
where all the moles
are sea slugs

Robin D. Gill has gathered 21 historical haiku about moles being beaten or pitted against sea cucumbers. In an act he calls mole exorcism, farmers would drag a sea slug by a string across a field 'because moles were believed to hate the smell of sea slug!'[34] As such, in Japanese folklore, *namako* – the sea slug – is the natural nemesis of the mole, whom gardeners there loathe as much as they do anywhere else in the world. Gill notes of the above poem, 'Moles in the Sinosphere were known to turn into quail and vice versa; this is the only instance I know where mole turns sea slug.'[35] He posits several explanations for this metaphor of transformation into the enemy – from islands looking like molehills poking out of the sea to the mutual blindness of moles and sea slugs – but settles on the probability that the specific island in question was both a habitat for moles and shaped like a sea cucumber. One wonders, could 'sunrise island' (*asahi* means sunrise) be a seventeenth-century reference to the tiny isle of

Uotsuri-jima in the Senkaku Islands, home to the Ryukyu mole?[36] The island, viewed on satellite maps, certainly has the proper shape.

Gill also shares a Japanese folk tale in which mole and sea slug face off:

> A cruel stepmother mistreats two sweet sisters, Moon and Star. God mercifully takes them up to heaven, putting them in the firmament while turning the cruel stepmother into a mole who cannot even see the sun, and lets their lonely father see them on the day of the first full moon of the New Year, when they descend to the shore of the sea. The sea cucumber serves to keep the hated stepmother at bay that day because she hated them.[37]

Transformation into a mole comes as punishment for an evil stepmother. Cosmology is at work in the story, providing a creative explanation of the year's first full moon. While the stepmother mole is unable to see the sun any longer, banished from appreciating its light, she nevertheless continues to pose a threat to the strained relationship between her husband and his daughters. That a sea slug slides in to keep her distracted during the bittersweet family reunion is the kind of localized cultural detail that makes studying folklore from around the world so much fun. How often does one hear about the heroic actions of a sea cucumber?

In a story widespread on the Korean peninsula, 'a mole father seeks the most powerful being in the world as a husband for his beautiful daughter, only to learn from the huge, wise, old statue called the Mireuk that moles are the most feared and respected of creatures.'[38] Mireuk is a beneficent creator god who is later tricked out of his peaceful rule by Seokga, a malevolent god. Statues of Mireuk became common throughout Korea between the tenth

A mole and a hedgehog meet in this French illustration from the 1800s.

and fourteenth centuries. In this story, Mireuk's goodness comes through one of these statues to advise a power-hungry father mole as to the best sort of match for his daughter. We know from biology that male moles are absent fathers, having nothing whatsoever to do with raising their young. Yet here the animal cast as the stifling, overinvested father is a mole. By revealing that moles are so feared and respected, essentially playing to the father's desires for his daughter's match, the Mireuk instils in him a sense of dignity with regard to his own kind: the perfect husband for his beautiful mole daughter is a mole groom. As opposed to the earlier Ainu story of marriage, there is no violence perpetrated here, the focus being the misguidedness of the father's aspirations for his daughter's life.

Shifting to the Occident, there exists in Hebrew culture a common story known as 'The Mole and the Well', which is included in Talmudic traditions. In it a maiden lowers herself into a well to get a drink of water and cannot pull herself out again.

A man finds her and she agrees to marry him if he pulls her up, which he does. Seeking to bind their covenant, she sees a mole pass by and tells him, 'Heaven, this mole, and this well will be witnesses that we do not lie to each other.'[39] After sharing her bed, however, he abandons her and returns to the city, where he marries another woman. Their first child is born and a mole strangles it. A second son is born and he falls into a pit. His wife demands to know why such bad fortune befalls their family, so he tells her about the woman and their covenant. She divorces him and he returns to the first woman, who, in his absence, has suffered from epilepsy. When he recounts to her the mole and the well, they reconcile. Cured of her affliction, they go on to attain wealth and have many sons. Admiel Kosman reads the mole's presence in the story as symbolic of the oath taken by the man and woman:

> On the one hand, it symbolizes the faith that is represented by the maiden: digging in the dark is a suitable metaphor for her situation, from the beginning of the tale to the salvation that comes in its end . . . On the other hand, the mole symbol has a negative function here. The man is the mole, who, in dark ways, undermines the spiritual truth.[40]

Romanians give the mole great significance, including it in a creation story in which it asks God if it can help with creating the world from a ball of thread. God consents, letting the mole hold the thread from which the Earth is woven. The mole suffers self-doubt though, and gives up after thinking it has let out too much slack. Embarrassed and abandoning the unfinished project, it burrows underground, where it is said to still hide from God to this day. However, in this story God is not upset with the mole at all and sends a bee to find him with a message: 'God just wanted the mole's advice on how to correct the mistake.'[41] The bee finds the mole and delivers this message, but the mole is incredulous of his own abilities to help the Creator. Unwilling to return to God without good news, the bee eavesdrops and hears the mole mumbling to itself its thoughts on how it will solve the problem. '"I would squeeze the earth," it said, "yes, squeeze it and make it smaller. Then there would be mountains, of course, and valleys, too. But that smaller earth would fit underneath heaven."'[42] Flitting back to God, the bee offers up what it has heard. The Creator gives it a try, squeezing the mess of thread, and what the mole reckoned comes to pass; all of the Earth fits into place beautifully.

The mole appears in relation to death again in stories of the Low Countries, playing a minor role as a gravedigger in tales of Reynard the Fox. Among Germans, moles have a folkloric kinship with dwarves. In *Thus Spoke Zarathustra*, Friedrich Nietzsche's late nineteenth-century philosophical novel, the protagonist's arch-enemy is 'half dwarf, half mole, lame, making lame, dripping lead into my ear, leaden thoughts into my brain'.[43] This half-mole antagonist is the hero's opposite, drawing him downward in an alchemical process towards perfected knowledge. Writer Richard Dehmel, who influenced Kafka's tales of human-to-creature metamorphosis, is best remembered for his story 'Das Märchen vom Maulwurf' (The Fairy Tale of the Mole). Published in 1896, it tells of a dwarf king who, bored with his seven rooms encrusted in precious gems, yearned for a light that would combine them all into one. All the dwarves thought he had gone mad but he set about digging upward, to the earth's surface, with his fingers. After 3,000 years, his fingers raw, he considered turning back. Convinced his people would lock him away in a madhouse, he instead dug for another 3,000 years.

W. KAULBACH, PINX   J. McGOFFIN, SCULP

Gravedigger
moles, lower
left, in tales
of Reynard
the Fox,
19th century.

Finally breaking through, he was astonished to find 'there were
so many colors up there, as if a thousand colorful knives were
stinging his heart.'[44] Staring into the sun's radiance, he was
blinded. Falling back down the hole he dug, his nose sharpened
and fright fused his black velvet cape to his body. According to
this story, 'that's why [moles] have a black velvet coat and pink
dwarf hands and are blind.'[45]

88

For Dutch author Wil Huygen and artist Rien Poortvliet, who popularized wee folk in red caps with their best-selling book *Gnomes* (1976), 'Moles are good friends of the gnome.'[46] Moles are entrusted with digging the shafts for both sewage and wells in a gnome home. This positive regard for moles, however, is rather atypical in fairy tales. For famed Danish fairy-tale writer Hans Christian Andersen, a mole stands as the ugly, tiresome, imposed fiancé of the titular character in his 1835 tale 'Tommelise', known in most English translations as 'Thumbelina'. The heroine, an inch-tall girl born from the heart of a tulip blossom, finds herself beset by matchmakers and would-be grooms who, without any respect for her wishes, see her as prime wife material. A mother toad abducts her with the aim of wedding her to her son, a cockchafer carries her away for himself until he tires of her, and when at last she seems to find a friend in a field mouse, the rodent sets her up with her wealthy neighbour: a mole.

Andersen works with the animal's actual features to present a dour, fusty bachelor with nothing whatsover in common with the tiny woman he should like to marry. His black velvet coat is a symbol of his wealth. His underground home is noted by the mouse as being twenty times bigger than her own, containing a drawing room, a kitchen – and a larder, which we know moles actually keep. He is also, in stereotypical fashion, blind, though Andersen uses this as an opening for him to fall in love with Tommelise through the sound of her voice when she sings for him. Though his heart swells for her, he does not show it due to his own antisocial nature. He is also a complainer, bemoaning flowers, even though he has never even seen them, and nice weather: 'Every evening the mole came visiting, but all he talked about was how nice it would be when the summer was over. He didn't like the way the sun baked the earth; it made it so hard to dig.'[47] The character is thoroughly mole-some, the author tweaking biological traits in the service of caricature. This mole is the quint-essential conservative bore, a stand-in for the potential dreariness of 'marrying up'.

It is worth considering the field mouse's judgement in playing matchmaker. She tells Tommelise that if she can get the mole to make her Mrs Mole, she will be well provided for. Here we have a thoroughly unromantic perspective on marriage, one that is historically based, by which unions are viewed as opportunities for maximizing resources. The field mouse projects onto the girl the old tradition of arranged marriage, of which Tommelise wants no part. She represents a turn towards the romantic and the notion that a woman may have legitimate desires of her own that are worth pursuing. When she comes to a frozen swallow lying prone in the tunnel to the mole's home, the mole bids her to ignore it – but that is precisely what she cannot do. She kisses its eye, the bird revives and she cares for it in secret all winter. She lets him go in spring, a cause for misery, but on her wedding day to the mole the following autumn, just as she is bidding farewell to the sun in forfeit to a subterranean marriage, the swallow returns. He carries her off to a happy ending, in which she falls in love with the tiny king of the flower angels, presumably one of her own kind. The mole never re-enters the story. We can only assume that he is left waiting at the altar, not knowing why he has been stood up, perhaps even blindly certain that she is simply running late. Andersen's mole is a stand-in for the rich suitor who lacks vitality and charm: an undesirable creature, one for which a genuine love is unthinkable.

This perspective is lent added menace in the 1994 animated film adaptation, *Thumbelina*, directed by Don Bluth and Gary Goldman. English actor John Hurt provides the voice of Mr Mole. Taking liberties with Andersen's classic fairy tale, with musical interludes in the mould of Disney, Mr Mole is given far more power than he possesses in the original. He wears golden spectacles, an Elizabethan ruff and carries an orb-topped cane, all symbols of Old World wealth. This mole is more a stereotypically villainous count, sporting pointy goatee and frou-frou attire, than the mole of the original tale, who is stuffy and boring. He even pays Mrs Fieldmouse in gold to enlist her help in persuading Thumbelina to marry him. Voiced by Carol Channing, the field mouse is made more troublesome as well, exhibiting an alarming capacity for passive aggression when guilt-tripping Thumbelina into the engagement. Mrs Fieldmouse's big number, 'Marry the Mole', before devolving into brassy burlesque, has her invoking the economic folly of marrying for love. The tune won songwriter Barry Manilow a Razzie Award for Worst Original Song.[48] We find here a dearth of love for the mole – at the levels of characterization, songwriting (being a throwaway tune by the undeniably talented Manilow) and critical recognition.

For all that, *Thumbelina* is a glowing adaptation of Andersen's story when compared to the one that interrupts the plot of low-budget flop *Santa and the Ice Cream Bunny* (1972). In this version, filmed in live action with shoddy costumes, the field mouse is also a mole and Thumbelina's engagement to her neighbour is forged on a basis of common loneliness. Mr Digger is an unhappy gentleman in an overcoat, with an accent from the Bronx. The movie's poor production quality made it a natural choice for pillory by the RiffTrax comedians who crack jokes over the soundtrack. When Mr Digger pitches marriage, Bill Corbett jokes, 'And hey, at least I'm not one of those types of moles where their nose looks like an anus!'[49] In animation, B-movie treatment and comic roast, Andersen's mole is consistently portrayed on the screen as unappealing in character. As seen over and over again, moles are derided as suitors, but the turn to film has exaggerated their undesirable qualities to grotesque ends.

Mr Mole offers
Thumbelina flowers,
artist unknown,
late 1800s.

Elsa Beskow's art
for 'Thumbelina',
1920.

One of the most curious finds in mole folklore was dug up by zoologist Rob Atkinson, recovering from obscurity 'The First Cornish Mole' (1870). Written by Robert Stephen Hawker, whom Atkinson describes as 'the compassionate, eccentric, opium-smoking rector of Morwenstow', the Cornish story is subtitled 'A Morality from the Rocky Land'.[50] It tells the tale of Alice of

A Mole.

See, chil-dren, the mis-guid-ed Mole.
He lives down in a deep, dark hole;
Sweet-ness, and Light, and good Fresh Air
Are things for which he does not care.
He has not e-ven that make-shift
Of fee-ble minds — the *so-cial gift.*
But say not that he has no soul,
Lest hap-ly we mis-judge the Mole;
Nay, if we mea-sure him by Men,
No doubt he sits in his dark den
In-struct-ing oth-ers blind as he
Ex-act-ly how the world *should* be.

the Combe, who worships her own beauty in a robe of woven velvet and is damned in a blinding light for rejecting others' plans for her life, casting aside her mother's prayer for her to wed Sir Beville of Stowe. Alice vanishes and is later found by the priest of Morwenna, who 'heard and understood voices in the air when spirits speak and glide'[51]: 'Therefore her rich array had been changed into the skin of a creeping thing; and her large proud eyes were sealed up, and she herself had become THE FIRST MOLE OF THE HILLOCKS OF CORNWALL!'[52] Thereafter, the tale becomes a lecture to young women instructing them to refrain from vanity in their apparel and using their eyes to allure men. Many today will find in this legend a hefty dose of misogyny and patriarchal attitudes that, though outworn, persist. Again, transformation into a mole is depicted as a punishment for a woman displaying rising agency.

Moles can also be found in the folklore of the descendants of Europeans who settled across North America. 'If I's a mole in the ground,' goes an old folk song out of North Carolina, 'I'd root that mountain down.'[53] Two nineteenth-century fables shared by whites and blacks in Maryland speak to why moles are the way they are by offering human scenarios. In one, 'the mole was an over-proud young lady . . . condemned to travel underground as a punishment for her pride.'[54] In the other, the animal made a bad bargain:

> Once the mole had eyes like other animals, but no tail. He met a creature which ridiculed him for his poverty in this latter respect. The derision preyed on his mind, and, when he met a being who could help him, he petitioned for aid. He was told that he must give up his eyesight[,] 'So he sold his eyes for his tail.'[55]

Yet again moles are used to negatively depict shortcomings common among people, in these instances vanity and rash decisions made on the basis of low self-esteem.

In the Ozarks of Missouri, a tale about a young couple features a moleskin changing the direction of their love life. When Betsey is reluctant to have sex with her boyfriend, 'preferring instead to satisfy his urges manually', he cites a local belief 'that if a man doesn't have regular intercourse, his penis will turn into a wild animal'.[56] Betsey, a schoolteacher, tells him this is merely a legend

'A Frightful Apparition', magazine illustration from the late 1800s.

with no basis in reality. He visits an old woman for advice, Gram French, who 'tells the man to kill a mole and skin it, and to place the skin over his penis, face and teeth at the tip, next time he and Betsey are together'.[57] He does, telling Betsey he has to see a doctor to get it treated. She is so shocked that she rethinks the strict limits she has placed on their physical relationship. Kate Stockton Kelley notes that this story from the 1800s and early 1900s, which would have been freely told in front of children, provides 'insights into the changes of gendered relationships with the onset of modernity'.[58] She argues that the deception at play, while unseemly by today's standards, 'was seen, on balance, as an ethically acceptable act'.[59] Missouri lore also suggests 'the dried skin of a mole, stuck fast to the chest with honey, will prevent or even cure asthma . . . Women sometimes wear a mole skin, or the dried foot of a mole, between their breasts in the belief that it prevents cancer.'[60] And so we find accounts of both men and women fetishizing the remains of moles, a tradition that is not limited to the Ozarks.

Parts of moles were long used in folk medicine across Europe. For example, in classical times Romans wore mole feet to ward

Mole paw amulets at the Science Museum, London.

off toothache. More recently, 'carrying a mole's forefoot in a pocket as an amulet to prevent cramp is a medical tradition specific to the East Anglian region of England. The feet were either hacked off a mole or bought from a shop.'[61] In Washington, DC, in the late 1800s, it was believed 'A mole's feet cut off and hung around a child's neck will help it in teething. In some instances in Virginia these odd amulets have been handed down . . . for generations.'[62] Much like carrying a rabbit's foot for luck, people have also fashioned charms from the limbs and organs of moles for occult purposes. One mole charm promised enhanced mental acuity and even prophecy, claiming 'if anyone shall swallow the heart of a . . . mole, while it is yet living and warm with natural heat, it improves his intellect, and helps him to remember, understand, and foretell things to come.'[63] Another tantalizes those seeking revenge and power over death:

> Whoever carries the hemlock herb, with the heart of a mole, on his person, vanquishes all his enemies, so that they will not be able to trouble him. Such a man will obtain much. When this herb is laid under the head of a sick person, the sick one, when he sings, will get well; if he cries, he will die.[64]

Hemlock, of course, is what the Athenians used to execute Socrates, so that fetish may best be left to the musty old books where it is recorded, for one's own safety – and that of the moles, of course.

5 Allegorical Moles

The psychologist C. G. Jung once invoked the trope of the sightless mole when explaining the typical limits of human consciousness:

> Our sight only reaches to a certain distance, our memory is insufficient, our perceptions are insufficient, and many things happen which we are too blind to see – blind moles . . . In our daily life in our overcrowded civilization, we have to be conscious, and so we become blind moles.[1]

That is, with regard to the way people muddle through the rush of modern life, Jung uses moles and their assumed blindness as the metaphor for all aspects of existence that people fail to detect. This association with blindness is probably the most common one ascribed to moles, even though many species of mole can see. Having considered the biology, mythology and folklore of moles, there is plenty to be gained now in considering the ways people invoke moles in their own lives. Indeed, there are many things we call moles in English, each of them connoting something distinct for the manners in which we conceive of moles conceptually.

The perfect way to dig into how we talk about moles is by considering the words people use for them. The word 'mole', according to the *Oxford English Dictionary*, is perhaps borrowed

from Old Frisian, Middle Dutch or Middle Low German. It may even be related to the Old Saxon word for lizard, *mol*, and the Old High German words for newt or salamander – *mol*, *molm* and *molt*. In English, the European mole used to be known as *mould-warp*, a name inherited from Germanic which translates to 'earth thrower'. Given the creature's distinctive habit of kicking up mole-hills, this metonym proved more popular than the Old English name *want*, itself likely a shortening of Middle Low German *wandworp* – again, for 'turner-over and thrower-up (of earth)'.

The Japanese word for mole, 土竜, translates to 'ground dragon'. This name is also given to the rice paddy eel, which crops up in the fields looking like a cross between a dragon and a worm. It may be that there is a folk explanation for calling them 'ground dragons' given the frequency of earthquakes in Japan and the behaviour of moles tunnelling underground. In French, the word for mole is *taupe*, from the Latin *talpa*. Today English speakers, probably unaware of its etymology, think of taupe as a colour. The reason for this definition goes back to fashion. At the turn of the twentieth century, Queen Alexandra, wife of King Edward VII of the United Kingdom, popularized moleskin as a stylish garment material in an effort to control the mole population in Wales. When the queen made it publicly known that she had ordered a moleskin muff, 'Immediately every other woman wanted a muff of the same.'[2] Prior to this, it had been a popular material for pocket-sized tobacco bags.[3] The harvesting of mole pelts, cut into rectangles and sewn together to make high-society coats, countered what was seen as the nuisance of moles on the land. Soon

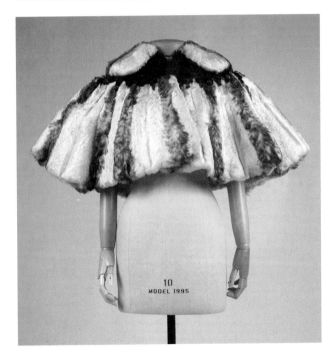

Feather and moleskin ensemble by C. C. Shayne, 1895.

merchants were using *taupe* to describe fabrics, the *OED* tracing its earliest recorded use to a Canadian newspaper describing colours of silk in 1911. In the world of fashion and interior design, those doing the selling favoured *taupe*, perhaps because *mole-coloured* lacks a certain panache.

To confuse matters, there are the false moleskins. One of them is a fustian garment material that is 'a heavy woven cotton with the pile cut off'.[4] The earliest use of the term cited in the *OED* is from 1792, attributed to an order for nearly 7 metres (7½ yards) of the fabric placed by the first American president, George Washington. In the nineteenth century, the French were among the first to wear 'moleskin pants and aprons to protect themselves from molten metal', with moleskin becoming a popular workwear in industry.[5] Today it is considered more of a dandified fabric, used in men's upscale trousers and jackets. While not made of mole skins, running one's palm across it will quickly reveal why it got its name; like their fur, it is soft and velvety on one side. This fabric has been used not only for clothing but bandages and the soundproofing of microphones. The other faux moleskin is the Moleskine, an Italian-designed notebook fashioned after those used by artists and writers such as Vincent van Gogh, Pablo Picasso, Ernest Hemingway and Bruce Chatwin. Many wonder whether their covers, given the brand's name, are a thin leather harvested from moles, but the *Los Angeles Times* reports, 'They're made from cardboard and oilcloth and not from dead moles.'[6] No moles were harmed in the making of those fashionable mole-skin clothes and Moleskine notebooks.

The most common homonym for 'mole' in English is what the *OED* defines as 'a spot or blemish on the skin'; having different roots, no etymological relationship exists between this meaning and that of burrowing animals. There is also the mole that is a pier or breakwater of stone, often in a harbour; it too bears no

Taxidermy scullery maid mole.

Card of Hanna Barbera's Morocco Mole cut from a box of bubble bath.

relation to the talpids. But what about the sort of mole involved in espionage, an embedded spy who leaks confidential information from inside an organization? Most certainly, the *OED* confirms that this sense of the word, that of being a double agent, is absolutely associated with fossorial mammals. The earliest recorded use is from 1922, and cartoon-lovers will recall one such character from *Secret Squirrel* (1965). Playing off contemporary espionage anxieties, Morocco Mole wears a fez and talks like Peter Lorre, parodying the actor's character Inspector Slimane in the international crime musical *Casbah* (1948). The author John

le Carré, however, is the person credited with popularizing the term during the Cold War in his novel *Tinker Tailor Soldier Spy* (1974). 'A mole,' he wrote, 'is a deep penetration agent so called because he burrows deep into the fabric of Western imperialism.'[7]

Le Carré, a former spy himself, had plenty of recent historical material to go on. Kim Philby, a British intelligence agent who defected to the Soviet Union in 1963, exemplifies the mole in this sense. Philby's spying career is most astonishing, given that he 'set up MI6's section to spy on the Soviet Union to which he was loyal'.[8] Unremorseful about betraying Britain, he once advised those attending a lecture in East Berlin that his best advice was simply, 'Deny everything.'[9] Another mole, Major Pyotr Popov, worked with the U.S. Central Intelligence Agency (CIA) to leak Soviet military secrets to the United States between 1953 and 1958. Yet another, Robert Philip Hanssen, was a Federal Bureau of Intelligence (FBI) counter-intelligence agent who sold American secrets to the Russians from 1979 to 2001, when he was caught. Clearly no nation has the better of the others when it comes to both employing and rooting out moles, seeing how all seem to have suffered and benefited from their presence.

In his book about Popov, William Hood states 'Mole is . . . so apt an expression' for describing a penetration agent, but he leaves its associations to the imagination.[10] The most obvious similarities include the habits of working below the surface, industriousness and evading entrapment to the great frustration of those on the hunt. David A. Vise describes Hanssen as 'a mole rummaging about' and a 'mole lurking',[11] but perhaps the strongest correlation between literal and metaphorical moles has to do with their shared vulnerability to greater forces. In another sense, both are antisocial at heart; in serving one country's intelligence agency by secretly serving in another's, one's inner life must be isolated and solitary. Idealism may be cited to suggest

Mole graffiti,
Prague, 2006.

internationally duplicitous behaviour is all for a bigger cause, but one could also argue that being a mole is incredibly self-serving. Another convicted CIA officer turned KGB mole, Aldrich Ames, admitted 'with a smirk that while he worked alone and did not know specifically of any moles himself, that didn't mean that other spies weren't around'.[12]

It is interesting that these people are labelled moles by those who loathe them as traitors, who are exasperated by their elusive presence in their midst – the term was not coined by double

agents describing themselves – suggesting that an implicit preju-
dice against actual moles exists. In the late 1980s and early 1990s,
Richard Davies fronted the Moles, an Australian psychedelic
indie-rock band that became a u.s.-based project. Being led by
an Australian expat, we might assume that the Moles were
named after marsupial moles – but no. Davies explains that he
named them for morally motivated spies from tv shows like
Get Smart (1965–70): 'That's the way the Moles were supposed
to be, an intelligent punk band, which is not a very popular
thing to be.'[13] Glancing towards the literary world, Indian author
Ashokamitran's book *Mole!* (2005) is a wry series of observations
made during his attendance at the International Writing Program
at the University of Iowa in the 1970s. Translator N. Kalyan Raman

stretched the meaning of its original title in Tamil, *Otran*, from 'spy' to 'mole'. In the Afterword, A. R. Venkatachalapathy asks, 'who is the mole? By constantly judging and understanding one society/culture in terms of the other, whom is [Ashokamitran] informing on? Is he informing on American culture to a Tamil audience? Or is it the other way around?'[14] Indeed, this question dominates the discourse around moles: who *are* they? That so little is known about the animals that live in our gardens may play into their metaphorical identity as double agents.

Another variant meaning of mol, as described in the *Oxford English Dictionary*, is a unit of measurement in chemistry: 'the quantity of specified elementary entities (molecules, ions, electrons, etc.) that in number equals the number of atoms in 0.012 kilogram of the carbon isotope of mass 12'. This mole, of course, is a simple shortening of the word 'molecule', though plenty of students of basic chemistry will recollect their instructor using the burrowing animal as a mnemonic for initially learning the term. In the 1980s Margaret Christoph, a science teacher at St

Internet meme featuring Amedeo Avogadro with chemistry's 'mole'.

Mark's High School in Wilmington, Delaware, took it as far as celebrating Mole Day every 23 October. She chose the date because it corresponds to the number of particles contained in a mole, which is 10^{23}. Along with demonstrations, contests and guest speakers, Mole Day also had its own mascots: 'We display Mr. Maxi Mole and Ms. Mille Mole (who are stuffed animals) in their house at 22.4 Mole Hole Lane.'[15] The number of atoms or molecules in a mole is known as Avogadro's number, named for chemist Amedeo Avogadro (1776–1856), who is sometimes pictured with a mole in Internet memes.

Given the preponderance of moles in Britain, it should not surprise anyone that there are places named for them. In England there are three villages called Mole – in West Sussex, Surrey and Devon – as well as Molehill Green in Essex, Molescroft in the East Riding of Yorkshire, Molesden in Northumberland and Molesworth in Cambridgeshire. Historically, Molesworth appears in tax records as far back as 1086 listed under the name Molesworde, having at that time one manor owing an annual rent to the lord of £4.[16] Nearly 1,000 years later, it is a small but affluent village sitting astride RAF Molesworth, an airbase with its roots in the First World War. My grandfather Norbert Gronert was stationed there during the Second World War, serving as one of the first B-17 radar technicians in the 303rd 'Hell's Angels' Bombardment Group. In 2015, the U.S. Air Force and Royal Air Force announced their intention to abandon the base and sell the land sometime between 2020 and 2023, potentially opening it to housing.[17] Visiting Molesworth today, one finds at its heart a charming signpost featuring the church, a tractor, crossed keys, a dog watching a man and woman playing croquet – and a pince-nez-wearing mole waving from a molehill. Whether or not moles had much to do with the place's naming, their part in the community has clearly been embraced by the parish council.

Village signpost in Molesworth, England.

Moles rarely appear in military history but, during the Vietnam War, the American military built Mole City, a patrol base set up in rice paddies south of Tây Ninh: 'Mole City got its name because almost everything except a lookout tower and the kitchen was at least partially underground.'[18] Its purpose was to offer a small support base in close proximity to the North Vietnamese Army (NVA), built to draw them into a trap: 'It was tiny, barely 100 yards [91 m] across in any direction. Circular in nature and positioned but a couple of clicks from the Cambodian border, it would prove to be the ultimate lure. It would have a defending force of 500 men made up of three companies of the [4th Battalion, 9th Infantry] "Manchus".'[19] A sign outside the barbed wire perimeter read:

WELCOME

to

MOLE CITY

THE SANDBAG CAPITAL OF THE WORLD

Sign erected
outside Mole City,
Vietnam, 1968.

WELCOME
to
MOLE CITY
THE SANDBAG CAPITAL OF THE WORLD

Four days after construction began on Mole City, it was attacked:

> During the early morning hours of December 22, 1968,
> Mole City came under a massive ground assault by the
> 272d Regiment of the 9th NVA Division. During the battle,
> the 4th Battalion of the 9th Infantry Manchus killed 106
> enemy. The attack began shortly after midnight with a
> fierce mortar, 75mm recoilless rifle and RPG [rocket-
> propelled grenade] attack which was followed immediately
> by a heavy concentration of small arms and automatic
> weapons fire . . . 'In my 26 years of service,' [said Colonel
> Robert L.] Fair, 'I've never seen a fight like this one.'[20]

John Senka's account of the seven-hour battle at Mole City and
his rescue after being wounded is harrowing: 'The most beautiful
sight I've ever seen was when a black Mortar Sergeant poked his

head into our blackened grave and rejoiced, "There are some Americans alive in here."'[21] One thing that sets the 'Manchus' apart from other people associated with moles is the way they wholeheartedly took to the metaphor of Mole City. People do not normally associate themselves with moles; typically there are certain conditions, often unfavourable, that lead people to identify *others* with moles.

In her book *The Mole People: Life in the Tunnels beneath New York City* (1993), Jennifer Toth shared her experiences interacting with homeless people living along abandoned railways under the surface of Manhattan. Says former Metropolitan Transportation Authority maintenance inspector Norman Diederich, 'There were talks that the moles were cannibals . . . That they could see in the dark. That they spoke their own language. Creepy stuff, straight out of a horror movie . . . Most was made-up.'[22] Not just another urban legend, Toth notes 'the term [mole people] is used . . . disparagingly, to establish higher status within the homeless community.'[23] Bernard Isaacs, who led a group living under Riverside Park, took it for a pejorative, 'a label that portrays

Wood mole sculpture at Ruby Wood, Peak District, England.

him as an animal, not as a person'.[24] Squeeze, another person who lived amid the pipes underground, accepted the name on the basis of what it said about the people who used it against them: 'let them call us the mole people, cuz that 'bout sums it up, how they view us and how they treat us. We are the mole people.'[25] Urging that we recognize their humanity, Toth insisted 'mole people don't exist beneath the surface of New York City, but people do.'[26] Efforts were made to give these people Section 8 housing units, but some returned to life underground. In 2015 Anthony Taille found people living in the same tunnels Toth had visited more than twenty years earlier. His assessment of their living conditions suggests they were worse off than their predecessors, who had organized their lives underground. 'The few Mole People left [in 2015],' according to Taille, 'survive in hurt.'[27]

While all of these connections are peculiar, they nevertheless affect how we think about the mole. Etymologically linked to their habits of 'throwing earth' and underground rumblings, the words used to name them reveal human estimation and imagination. The politics of identifying with or labelling other people as moles has spoken to conditions of war, anxieties and dynamics surrounding duplicitous espionage, and the diminished agency of the homeless. Even with the history of wearing real and cotton moleskin, patterns of meaning emerge with regard to fashion and class. Our metaphorical moles, it seems, say more about us than about their namesake.

6 Moles in Literary and Popular Culture

When it comes to the arts, rarely does the mole take centre stage. More often than not moles find representation as supporting characters, filling cameo roles in stories and illustrations in which the stars are other species considered more charismatic or compelling. Is the marginalization of the mole in popular culture related to the fact that moles are so rarely seen, even when people have them living in their gardens? Their submerged presence in art and storytelling, mirroring their relationship to people in real life, has become thematic in how they are portrayed. As such, it's a surprise when moles receive sustained attention in a literary or popular work, for suddenly audiences have a chance to think closely about an animal they have failed to think much about before.

Take the plays of Shakespeare, where moles, while mentioned peripherally, are never the topic of a soulful soliloquy. When his dead father's voice pleads from the stage floor that he swear silence by his sword, Hamlet says, 'Well said, old mole! Canst work i' th' earth so fast? A worthy pioneer!' (1.5.915–16) In *The Tempest*, beastly Caliban advises Stephano and Trunculo to 'tread softly, that the blind mole may not / Hear a foot fall.' (IV.1.1937–8) Shakespeare wrote of moles or molehills eight times in his plays, often referring to their assumed blindness, occasionally employing the word as an insult. To be called a blind mole in Elizabethan drama was to be labelled a hopeless idiot. The bard also invoked them in association with mysterious forces and black magic. In *Henry IV, Part 1* Prince Hal's rival, Hotspur, singles out the mole as one of the ridiculous, esoteric topics his father, Glendower, rambles on about: 'sometimes he angers me / with telling me of the mouldwarp and the ant' (III.1.1693–4) – *mouldwarp* being an old word for 'mole', as we saw in the last chapter.

Two centuries later, Romantic poet William Blake honoured the creature as a possessor of unique knowledge. 'Thel's Motto', accompanying *The Book of Thel*, grants that the mole holds chthonic knowledge a bird of prey can never know:

> Does the Eagle know what is in the pit?
> Or wilt thou go ask the Mole:
> Can Wisdom be put in a silver rod?
> Or Love in a golden bowl?[1]

The poem, dated 1789, is often interpreted as an expression of disillusionment with the Church of England. This motto was composed almost as a postscript, Blake giving it a plate of its own following the first five of the poem. Though the eagle may never know the depths of the pit, the mole will never know soaring heights; both animals emerge as rather one-sided in their individual knowledge. The figure of Thel, a young woman struggling to understand why youth must end, could potentially learn what the eagle and mole each have to share. The urgency of her motto comes in the act of asking not only the high-flying bird of prey but the lowly mole, acknowledging that a better understanding of wisdom and love will come from consulting both creatures instead of just one. In Blake's estimation, though Thel fails to live up to her own motto, human beings are capable of incorporating both varieties of understanding, thereby achieving a comprehensive knowledge with which to face life's highest and lowest conditions.

The American poet Theodore Roethke answered Blake in 'The Pit', the second part of his 1948 poem 'The Lost Son': 'Who stunned the dirt into noise? / Ask the mole, he knows.'[2] In deferring to the mole, 'The lost son is instructed to look downward, to dig into nether regions of psychic history for answers to his questions.'[3] Roethke's poetic alter ego 'plunges into the depths of the pit himself, into the region of the subconscious, to gain knowledge of the hidden'.[4] Given the rise of psychology, Roethke consciously turns to the mole as an animating figure imagined to be completely at home in the unconscious. Later seeking symbols for the bipolar disorder he lived with, his 1963 poem 'The Abyss' presents the poet becoming a mole: 'I'm no longer a bird dipping a beak into rippling water / But a mole winding through earth.'[5] The poet splits the bird and the mole into an either/or binary. If the bird represents the heights of mania and the mole the depths of depression, he is unable to balance their ways, instead transforming from one into the other. Here the abyss of psychological darkness takes over completely, mental illness being presented as a transmogrifying condition that can turn one from man to bird to mole.

While Blake was the first to honour the mole as a spiritual seeker and Roethke deepened that sense of the animal, no one has developed this trope more strikingly than writer, director and actor Alejandro Jodorowsky. The most enigmatic mole of all, in any artistic representation to date, is the central character in the 1970 surrealist Western film *El Topo* (Spanish for 'The Mole'). In the title sequence Jodorowsky narrates a brief, three-sentence fable: 'The mole digs tunnels under the earth, looking for the sun. Sometimes, he gets to the surface. When he sees the sun, he is blinded.'[6] This is spoken over black-and-white still images,

DISTRIBUZIONE
STEFANO FILM
UNA ESCLUSIVA P.D.A.
EL
TOPO
DI ALEXANDRO JODOROWSKY
TECHNICOLOR
PRODOTTO DA ALLEN KLEIN PER LA ABKCO FILM

coloured in crayon, of what appear to be a mongoose, a vole, a nutria, what may be a ringtail possum or a potto, and human hands digging in soil. That Jodorowsky does not use a picture of a mole while imparting the opening parable should not surprise anyone who watches the film, for it is one of the most bizarre movies ever made, presenting the dreamlike and blood-soaked adventures of a soul-seeking gunfighter in Mexico. Jodorowsky mashed up genres decades before the practice became mainstream, cross-pollinating the Western with spirituality, black comedy and the avant-garde.

El Topo is a black-clad anti-hero who abandons his young son and works to impress a woman by duelling the four best gunmen in the desert. Shot down by the woman and her lover, he is healed by a group of disabled outcasts trapped in a cave. Their matriarch, making a meal of beetles, chooses him to dig the tunnel that will free her people to life above ground. Bleached white from head to toe and sworn to help them after abandoning his life of killing, he goes about trying to aid his healers. Transgressive imagery, absurdity, desperation and graphic violence ensue. Jodorowsky, considered one of cinema's great experimental visionaries, never shows us an actual mole in the film. This omission drives home the point that El Topo is a mole in abstract. The very mole-ness of his character is richly metaphorical, playing on the ancient trope of the mole's relationship with death, healing and mysteries lurking in the earth beneath us. Many film critics have expressed confusion and even bafflement at the Western's symbolism. 'What is El Topo seeking in the desert?' asks film critic Roger Ebert. 'Why, he is seeking symbols, images, bizarre people and events, with which to fill the film.'[7] Returning to the opening narration, this seeking is his life's task of tunnelling. Breaking through to the blinding surface, so to speak, is his sacrifice. Jodorowsky's mole digs through the spiritual side of life to

Italian poster for *El Topo* (1970).

integrate the opposites within and without, emerging from the dark depths of the unconscious into the illumination of enlightenment. Again the image of mole as a digger through life's journey is symbolically presented, though done in ways only thought of by an auteur as idiosyncratic as Jodorowsky.

Another great contributor to our sense that moles illustrate our own seeking of the sacred – and specifically an enlightenment of love – is the author William Horwood. More than any other writer in the world, Horwood has enriched what he calls 'moledom' in the imaginations of readers through his six-volume saga, told in two trilogies: *The Duncton Chronicles* and *The Book of Silence*. The cycle starts with *Duncton Wood*, published in 1980. Each book offers upwards of five hundred pages of operatic fantasy about moles living in relation to each other and a standing stone from which they draw their own cosmology. Beverly Jane Loo, who edited the first novel, explained, 'It is about good and evil, the search for God and the search for love.'[8] Horwood confirms the series found its beginning in love:

> The woman to whom *Duncton Wood* is dedicated said one day that she felt like a mole. I said, well, moles are small and black and you're blond and large and Californian. To which she replied, 'well I do feel like that so write me a story about a mole'. That's how *Duncton Wood* began.[9]

That Horwood's lover, the broadcaster and writer Leslie Kenton, spoke of feeling like a mole is an interesting occurrence on its own. Archetypal psychologist James Hillman, speaking of animals in dreams, said, 'they teach us something, but they're not part of us. They correspond with part of us.'[10] In imagining an animal as a part of nature with which one can connect, 'you have more respect for that part of yourself and you begin to try to live it right.'[11] In this instance, Horwood paid close attention to a sense Kenton had about herself, honouring *her* imagined 'moleness', and unfurled an astonishing expression of devotion that eventually resulted in six epics exploring a human side of moles. As Hulver, the first book's kindly elder, puts it, 'you'll find that if you give such a mole your help, or in other words your love, they will often repay you in ways you could never have dreamed of.'[12]

The Duncton moles are depicted in ways that lean towards honouring the biology of actual moles: they do not wear clothing, they dig tunnels, they sup on earthworms. They also talk, practise religious worship and live in communities under a social hierarchy. As such, while being mole-sized and displaying mole physiology, these moles are anthropomorphized, especially on an emotional level. The first book explores the tension between the tyranny wrought by abusive fathers and the lasting pain of loving them. Bracken and especially Rebecca are children of diabolical fathers, Burrhead and the evil Mandrake respectively. The characters find their destinies woven in direct relation to their fathers' cruelties, and readers are exposed to details of trauma as it manifests in children of violent men, as well as the traumas that shaped those men. Mandrake is shown to be a hulking mole whose murderous ways seem to stem from his own traumatic birth. *Duncton Wood*'s overbearing fathers do not reflect moles in nature – who never know or interact with their young – but they certainly, tragically, say plenty about human fathers. As fate would have it, the writer's father was a complete mystery to him. In the author's note to the final volume, closing fifteen years of writing about moles, Horwood acknowledged that his mother's death 'made it possible for me to find out who my father really was. I never knew him, nor his full name . . . *The Book of Silence* is about the long journey we all must make to come to terms and live beyond whatever enshadows our particular life.'[13] This fatherly absence, typical of the upbringing of a mole, casts the darkness that sustained the author's grandest artistic endeavour.

A variation on this theme of the mole being one on a quest is found in the realm of video games. Monty Mole was the hero of a series of games created by Peter Harrap for the Commodore 64 and zx Spectrum (1984–90). *Wanted: Monty Mole* was created in three months by nineteen-year-old Harrap at the height of the 1984–5 miners' strike in the UK. A two-dimensional platform game, one plays Monty Mole as he digs coal and dodges threats. Curiously political for a computer game, its 'final boss' is Scargill, then actual leader of the National Union of Mineworkers. Defeating him lands Monty in prison, a surprising outcome for winning a game. The blogger UnknownSubject notes, 'it is the miners who get screwed over no matter what they do. *Wanted: Monty Mole* takes a sympathetic, working-class position on a turbulent issue of its day.'[14] Typically, moles turn up as minor foes in video games, such as in the Super Mario Bros series by Nintendo. But more

Star-nosed
mole avatar
in *Second Life*.

120

recently, people interested in identifying as a mole have been able to do so through social media. Some users of the social-networking programme Second Life wander its online virtual world in avatars of cartoonish talpids. What draws a person to live out her online persona in the form of a leucistic mole that can emerge at will from a molehill? Second-lifer Loretta McGinnis says, 'The avatar is programmed to run underground. It's great for sneaking up on people.' There is your answer: the element of surprise, always such a crowd-pleaser.

Moles have not made a tremendous impact in the realm of poetry, but some notable poets have lent their perspectives to the creatures – almost exclusively when encountering their carcasses. A survey of moles in twentieth-century poetry reveals an entire hitherto unrecognized school of dead-mole poets. Scottish poet Andrew Young's 'A Dead Mole' (1939) sets the scene for those driven to lyricize them. Though 'strong-shouldered', his dead mole is found 'Buried within the blue vault of the air'.[15] The inversion of day-to-day habits between people and moles is brought out in

Loretta McGinnis and Hedgie Wonder banter in virtual Dublin in *Second Life*.

the idea that, while their lives play out underground and ours occur above ground, their dead are observed above ground while we bury ours underground. As such, the experience of finding a mole seemingly interred in the open, its carcass left to the elements, leads the reader to contemplate the mystery of people's bodies being laid to rest in the earth.

In 1959 Sylvia Plath composed 'Blue Moles', a poem in two stanzas that contemplates the discovery of two dead moles, 'shapeless as flung gloves', that have been chewed by a dog or fox.[16] Plath's journal entry for 22 October 1959 records the inspiration for this poem was two moles she found dead in the road: 'Dead, chewed of their juices, caskets of shapeless smoke-blue fur, with the white, clawlike hands, the human palms, and the little pointy corkscrew noses sticking up. They fight to the death Ted says. Then a fox chewed them.'[17] The Ted referred to is her husband, the fellow poet Ted Hughes; their tumultuous marriage ended tragically with Plath's suicide in 1963. In 'Blue Moles', it occurs to Plath that perhaps the two animals died in a duel, which correlates with the personal experience of a turbulent relationship in which fights break out nightly. Prefiguring Roethke's transformation in 'The Abyss', she imagines herself entering 'the soft pelt of the mole', drawing a comparison between moles' constant, subterranean eating of 'the fat children of root and rock' and her evening fights with her lover.[18] The blueness of their fur in the title resonates with blue as a shade of sadness and depression. 'Light's death to them,' she writes, 'they shrivel in it.'[19] One implication is that if this couple's arguments should stretch from night into daytime, they could very well finish each other off like the moles found dead in the lane: 'Blind twins bitten by bad nature.'[20]

'Star-nosed Mole' appeared in Pulitzer Prize-winner Anne Sexton's posthumous collection *45 Mercy Street*, published in 1976. Sexton prefaced the second section of the book, titled

'Bestiary U.S.A.', by saying 'I look at the strangeness in them and the naturalness they cannot help, in order to find some virtue in the beast in me.'[21] Strangeness befits the mole she examines. On the star-nosed mole's 'dear face' she saw a 'fifth hand', likening its Eimer's organs in the final line to Christ's cross.[22] Sexton's mole, 'angel-dog of the pit' in its 'sooty suit', has drowned at the edge of a pond.[23] Again, the pit proffered by Blake and Roethke returns. In this case, unfortunately, the creature making its home in the depths has succumbed at the thresholds of water and air. Sexton ennobles this mole, which could very well be one she actually happened upon, as a divine companion animal. In it she sees a fellow seeker, one who is at 'the end of the war'; this is all the more poignant given the poem's publication after Sexton's suicide.[24] Considering her announced intention of discovering the beast in herself, Sexton maps Christian virtue onto the dead mole, seeing a pietà in its lifeless form found in the marshy weeds.

Krtek stencil graffiti in Augsburg, Germany, 2013.

Her project doubles in purpose with this mole, for we catch her finding her own virtue in the beast.

The Nobel Prize-winning Irish poet Seamus Heaney ends 'Bone Dreams' in his 1975 collection *North* by finding a dead mole 'with the dew still beading on it'.[25] Section VI of the poem features a dead mole found in Devon. Heaney's Irish narrator, having never seen one before, 'had thought the mole / a big-boned coulter' – which is the part of a plough that leads in cutting a line in the soil – 'but there it was / small and cold / as the thick of a chisel'.[26] As we recall, moles are not native to Ireland, and so for this Irish poet the creature becomes a symbol of England. He is given an anatomy lesson, an unnamed speaker telling him to 'blow back the fur on his head' to see the 'points' that were its eyes.[27] Instructed then to touch its shoulders – the same feature mentioned in Young's poem – Heaney feels grass, grain and the Pennines, a range of hills in northern England. The dead Devonshire mole thereby becomes a relief map by which the foreign poet acquaints himself with England. The political, historical and cultural relationships between Ireland and Britain are marked by trauma, 'Bone Dreams' being an account of Heaney's sensuous attempts to know England against that backdrop. The dead mole reframes the Irish perception of England's magnitude, dropping the sense of English power from that of a plough to 'the thick of a chisel'.[28] Raphaël Ingelbien posits Ted Hughes 'may well be the interlocutor who invites Heaney to touch the mole'.[29] If so, Hughes played a part in inspiring two of the greatest dead-mole poems of all time.

The 1992 work 'Mole Totem' by English poet Graham Mort presents a gruesome spectacle: mole carcasses arranged along a fence line. This display is traditional practice among rural mole-catchers in parts of Britain and Europe. By hanging dead moles along a field's fence, the mole-catcher tallies an honest fee from the landowner. And yet the sight has the potential to bewilder or even dismay those who may suspect grim happenings other than pest control. Mort's poem describes the scene without explanation, lyricizing the cadavers' decomposition. Their 'bone flippers', left to the elements, are still poised to swim, the strychnine used to poison them washing from their spines with rain.[30] Their dangling, desiccated bodies are cast as holding the essence of soil-bound livelihood: 'airborne seeds of a subterranean will'.[31] The poem presents their remains returning to the earth from which they came as a natural process, suggesting that the way they decay shares qualities with the ways moles live. Mort's use of the word 'totem' in the title intrigues, given the word's Native American etymology. An Ojibwa or Algonquin word, the *Oxford English Dictionary* relates its meaning as 'that which marks the family or tribe'. Ancestry is inherent, suggesting that the practice characterized in 'Mole Totem' is emblematic of the people of northern England and perhaps even of the moles themselves.

Stephen Kettle's slate mole sculpture, Brecon Beacons, Wales, 2011.

One can turn to Pulitzer Prize-winner Mary Oliver in order to find a poem in which moles live, breathe and thrive. This distinctly positive regard for moles is no surprise, coming from the poet who asks, 'what is it you plan to do / with your one wild and precious life?'[32] In 'Moles', Oliver assures the reader that below what can be seen on the ground's surface, 'they're there', affirming their presence 'among the pale girders / of appleroot, / rockshelf '.[33] Instead of revealing the moles themselves, she points out the signs of their lifestyles, such as surface runs across the tops of fields: 'you can see the traceries / of their long / lonely walks.'[34] Oliver's moles are dignified creatures, 'so willing to continue' lives of hard labour in the deep, dark soil, 'finding it / delicious'.[35] Though we cannot see them, the case is made that moles lead lives worth living, that their existence is full of heavy lifting but is also pleasurable.

One more poem is worth mentioning: 'Mole' by Ted Hughes. Having played a crucial role in the dead-mole school of poets, Hughes himself only devoted a single poem to the mole, curiously since he was a decorated poet of wildlife. In 'Mole', a poem for children, Hughes assumes the identity of a living mole, narrating five stanzas from its point of view. The focus is primarily on the animal's features and peculiarities, each spun in a lyrical way. For instance, with regard to dining on worms, the mole finishes his poem with the guests with whom he shares meals: 'At my table sit / Centurion / And Ancient Brit.'[36] There is a bit of a riddle to the ending, particularly for young readers. Hughes's mole is relating his experience of inhabiting strata of earth that reflect Britain's history, specifically when the Romans ruled the island and, more vaguely, Neolithic people called it home. The British mole lives in layers of earth where historical and even prehistoric skeletons are buried. And so, while Hughes does not write of dead moles, he does write of one that dines with the dead.

Authors and artists have also viewed moles as mildly or absurdly curious inconsequentialities in the goings-on of human life. Noteworthy instances of moles appearing in literary fiction include D. H. Lawrence's 1912 short story 'Second Best', Franz Kafka's stories 'The Village Schoolmaster' – subtitled 'The Giant Mole' (1914) – and 'The Burrow', and Éric Chevillard's 2004 story 'Moles'. On the subject of cruelty to moles, Lawrence's 'Second Best' presents a pair of sisters who, while discussing men who have rejected them for other women, encounter a mole wandering above ground. After handling the mole and being bitten, Anne kills it with a stroke of her sister's walking-cane. '"Hasn't it got beautiful skin"', she suddenly says, 'stroking the fur with her forefinger, then with her cheek'.[37] The turn from brutality to appreciation unsettles the reader. Tom Smedley, a farmer who cites the damage moles do to his fields, is impressed by the dead specimen. At story's end, elder sister Frances delivers a second dead mole to him, through which an engagement is secured. With it comes the bittersweet disappointment of knowing she is 'off the market' and will not be able to marry another man, should one come along. And so, in an abstract way, Lawrence expresses the fairy-tale trope of moles and undesirable matrimony, in this case a second-best husband. Both dead moles serve a symbolically sacrificial purpose, putting to rest the sisters' expectations of whom they shall wed. A 1912 painting called *The Dead Mole*, contemporary with Lawrence's story, shares this theme of the inconsequentiality of moles in people's lives. Frederick Etchells's post-Impressionistic oil painting shows a man handing a dead mole to a boy beside a pond. Dabbed in greens, greys and blues with mauve accents, the pair's contorted poses and sickly complexions overwhelm the eye, so that the tiny mole is hardly noticeable. These works, where people think so little of killing moles, cast the characters harming them as being the true grotesques.

Kafka, renowned for his novella 'The Metamorphosis', iden-
tified with moles, writing to his friend Max Brod, 'We burrow
through ourselves like a mole, and emerge blackened and velvet-
haired from our sandy underground vaults, our poor little red
feet stretched out for tender pity.'[38] In 'The Village Schoolmaster',
widespread disregard for a schoolmaster's pamphlet on a giant
mole supposedly found in his Eastern European village has led
the narrator to write a pamphlet of his own, backing up its existence. The schoolmaster emerges as completely hostile to the
vindicating effort, however, the story being a study in interper-
sonal fumbles resulting from good intentions. The giant mole
never makes an entrance, though the schoolmaster is said to have
argued it was an astonishing *two yards long* when a disbelieving
scholar jokingly credited its alleged size to the local soil, providing
'the moles with particularly rich nourishment'.[39] The absurdity of
a cryptozoological mole is itself the joke, heightening the silliness
of disputes over unproven phenomena.

In Kafka's unfinished story 'The Burrow', however, readers
encounter the first-person machinations of a mole-like creature
as it racks its brain over the source of a low whistle heard throughout its tunnel system. The narrator never owns up to being a
mole, but its habits of filling larders, patrolling tunnels and
extending its burrow with new chambers all point to its true
identity. Though Kafka never finished it, the draft's stylistics
enhance the sense of being closed-in underground; the line rarely
breaks and one paragraph runs for seven pages. The pages upon
pages of block text are stitched through with anxiety-driven
speculations and plans that are worked and reworked. When
suddenly aware of the whistle heard throughout his home, the
narrator turns over what might have caused it and how to go
about repairing it. As such, a mole's worries about tunnel upkeep
are treated like human neuroses. Kafka presents a mole's

Molehills in the garden at author Thomas Hardy's cottage, Dorset, England.

consciousness as one dominated by a need for silence, food stores and a well-constructed home. Unhealthy human anxiety about survival and defence thus finds a voice when projected upon a mole perpetually fretting over the draftiness and safety of its burrow. 'I would be quite content,' it confides, 'if I could only still the conflict going on within me.'[40]

Éric Chevillard's story 'Moles' relates the bizarre pride of a neighbour of Samuel Beckett who, in childhood, relished tossing stunned moles into the Nobel-winner's garden. 'He lived right next door to Beckett,' the narrator gawps, 'and couldn't find anything better to do than toss moles into his yard.'[41] Instead of engaging the brilliant mind next door, this self-satisfied, grotesque character's '*only* source of entertainment' came in ruining the dramatist's

garden with abused moles lobbed over the fence. The narrator's thoughts unspool obsessively over the neighbour's earlier idiocy and cruelty and the effects they may have had on Beckett's work. Here, and in 'Second Best' and 'The Village Schoolmaster', moles accessorize significant happenings in the lives of human characters. Their reputation as a trifling yet sometimes maddening nuisance undermines each story's conflict in the service of humour. Even in 'The Burrow', the condition of persistent worry is treated as nonsensical. This sense is heightened because it emanates from a mole. Thematically, Lawrence, Kafka and Chevillard use the rather negative regard many people have for moles to bring readers closer to the inconsequentiality of so many of our own concerns.

The place where moles appear most often is in media aimed at children. Typically, moles have been used in storybooks and cartoons to illustrate qualities like friendship, anxiety, insecurity, hard work and a reasonable preference for solitude. The best-loved and most famous mole in all of literature is Mole in *The Wind in the Willows* by Kenneth Grahame. The 1908 novel is a classic of British children's literature, beloved around the world and adapted many times to various media, including an animated feature by Disney in 1949. Welcomed into the neighbourhood of the river by the more worldly Ratty, Grahame's Mole is a gentle homebody. This character, given as much to anxiety as he is to good cheer, has done a lot to soften public opinion about moles, who have long been seen as pests in Britain and Europe. He is a purveyor of 'animal-etiquette', an unspoken code of manners that places him on the polite side of the animal kingdom. Grahame's softened characterization of the creature proved instrumental in altering the way moles are depicted in the arts.

Mole resides at Mole End, a somewhat modest burrow he 'got through a windfall from an aunt'.[42] While better off in the past,

Paul Bransom's Mole in Kenneth Grahame's *The Wind in the Willows* (1913).

Mole is used to going without, though his forecourt is charmingly arrayed with a skittle alley, goldfish pond and 'brackets carrying plaster statuary – Garibaldi, and the infant Samuel, and Queen Victoria, and other heroes of modern Italy'.[43] Seth Lehrer calls it 'a catalog-bought Eden . . . decorated in the fashions of the late Victorian'.[44] For all the middle-class charm – curiously offset by sleeping-bunks in the wall – his dwelling sits neglected, shabby, 'the dust lying thick on everything'.[45] The only food to be found in the cupboards is sardines, captain's biscuits and a German sausage; from the cellar, Mole fetches bottles of beer to share with Rat. His home, abandoned from a spring clean when curiosity about the river took over, reveals Mole's interests in culture and creature comforts. It also speaks, 'with its spirit of divine discontent and longing',[46] to his loneliness and need of friendship. The relationships forged with Rat, Badger, Otter and Toad amplify with necessity once readers understand Mole has let his life go a bit.

Mole's vulnerability evokes sympathy, not just from readers but also his associates. Rat fetches Mole safely from the Terror of the Wild Wood, Otter cuffs a rabbit for giving Mole a hard time, and Badger compliments him on infiltrating the stoats that take over Toad Hall by disguising himself as a washerwoman. 'I perceive you have more sense in your little finger than some other animals have in the whole of their fat bodies,' Badger declares, 'You have managed excellently, and I begin to have great hopes of you. Good Mole! Clever Mole!'[47] Even Toad is said to be 'exceedingly jealous of Mole' for the stunt, it being 'exactly what he would have liked to have done himself, if only he had thought of it first'.[48] And yet Mole has traits we might ascribe to moles in general, being rather shy, timorous and quite harmless. In such a way, the sense that moles are antisocial animals is put to use in service of good character development, illustrating that these

qualities can be found in people, too. Though Mole is, by nature, a loner, he still benefits from having his dignity acknowledged by friends who accept him as he is.

A. A. Milne, author of *Winnie-the-Pooh*, challenged Grahame's storytelling logic, using the representation of Mole as his example:

In reading the book, it is necessary to think of Mole, for instance, sometimes as an actual mole, sometimes as a mole grown to human size, sometimes as walking on two legs, sometimes on four. He is a mole, he isn't a mole. What is he? I don't know. At least, I do know, and still I don't mind. He is a fairy, like so many immortal characters in fiction; and, as a fairy, he can do, or be, anything.[49]

Albert Borden Stridsberg took issue with the claim, arguing, 'Mr. Milne's critical passage . . . – belied by his own works – would suggest that fantasy is a-logical. A-logicality is incoherence.'[50] Illustrators have greatly affected the way the book is imagined, taking strikingly divergent tacks when depicting Grahame's characters. Paul Bransom, the first artist of *The Wind in the Willows*, portrayed the animals quite realistically, though his painting of Mole running on hind legs through the Wild Wood takes comic liberties. Nancy Barnhart, in illustrating the 1922 American edition of the book, dressed Mole and chums in gentlemanly attire. Probably the most memorable drawings of Mole were done by E. H. Shepard, who had illustrated Milne's Pooh books; his pen-and-ink line drawings accompanied a 1931 edition and were put together in conjunction with Grahame's input. Arthur Rackham's watercolours for a 1940 American edition of the book clothe Mole and give him spectacles while presenting his fur as scruffy and unkempt. Disney's 1949 film *The Adventures of Ichabod and Mr Toad*, a curious pairing of Washington Irving's 'Legend of Sleepy Hollow' and Grahame's *Wind in the Willows*, has not left the sort of visual stamp on Mole that their other adaptations have on storybook characters. Their fully animated Mole is not one of the studio's iconic character designs, his look and colour scheme being drab. *The Wind in the Willows* remains one of the most illustrated children's works of the twentieth century, the number of artists having brought forth their visions of Mole being too numerous to present here. It is also worth noting that *Duncton Wood* author William Horwood has written four additional books set in Grahame's world, carrying forward the adventures of Mole and friends.

Grahame's depiction of moles as affable and kindly can be felt in numerous moles since. Take Mole in the *Mole and Troll* (1972) series by Tony Johnston and Wallace Tripp. These are gentle

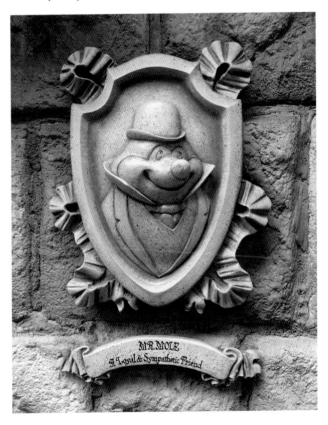

A stone carving of Mr Mole at Disneyland.

stories about friendship, birthday parties and days at the beach, the pairing of a mole with a mythological being coming down to the rhyming of their names. In the 1980s, Nickelodeon's children's programming included a TV show called *Pinwheel* that featured Molly McMole, a grandmotherly mole puppet who introduced cartoon shorts. Digger, in the animated series *Shirt Tales* (1982), is bashful, clumsy and endearing. (My first teddy as a child, actually, was Digger. I routinely fetched him from under my bed, where he often fell as I slept; as a child, it struck me as appropriate that he, as a mole, would seek it out as a dark, quiet place.) A fan of classical composer 'Molezart', Digger is defined mostly by his gentleness towards others. Additionally, *Fantastic Mr Fox* (2009), Wes Anderson's stop-motion adaptation of Roald Dahl's beloved book, features Phil the mole, a minor character voiced by James Hamilton. Phil, dressed in trousers held up by piano-key-patterned braces with an untied bowtie around his neck, minds can-and-string communications during the animals' orchestrated climactic retaliation against Boggis, Bunce and Bean. Though peripheral, he actually is appreciated for his natural skills; upon sharing his knack for seeing in the dark, Mr Fox says, 'That's incredible! We can use that!'[51] Instead of aligning with Hans Christian Andersen's take on moles as unsuitable bride-grooms, as encountered in 'Thumbelina' and its adaptations, these sweeter depictions can all be traced back to Grahame's achievement. Mole's literary descendants play up the notion of valuing others who may be smaller, shier and less outwardly confident in themselves.

The ancient belief that moles are blind also arises in stories for children. One such cartoon mole of the 1980s is Maulwurf, from an adaptation of stories by German children's author Janosch. The animated series *Janoschs Traumstunde* (Janosch's Dream Lesson) includes an episode, 'Grille und Maulwurf' (Cricket and

Mole), which is his retelling of 'The Ant and the Grasshopper'. Maulwurf is unable to see, drawn wearing large dark glasses and carrying a white cane. He also dons a yellow armband with three black dots on it, a symbol worn by the visually impaired in Germany to inform motorists and pedestrians. In Janosch's story, Maulwurf takes Grille the violinist in from the winter snow after others have rejected her. Their resulting closeness makes the story a fable about the good that can grow when we do not discriminate against those in need but do what we can to help them. The 2017 picture book titled *Mrs Mole, I'm Home!* by Jarvis, on the other hand, plays the idea that moles have bad eyesight for laughs. In its story, Morris digs his way home from work and ends up on different continents along the way. His misdirection is due to having forgotten that his glasses are on his forehead. Playing off the stereotype, this storybook revels in playful absurdity with colourful artwork and a happy ending that sees him arriving home.

Another kind of mole appearing in stories for children is the hero mole. Akin in some ways to the spirit-seeking moles encountered in Blake, Roethke, Jodorowsky and Horwood, these moles are intelligent makers of their own fate. Moldy Warp the Mole – playing on the old English word for mole – is the treasure-hunting star in Alison Uttley's Little Grey Rabbit series (1940). Another intelligent mole stars in perhaps the most irreverent tale about them, *The Story of the Little Mole Who Went in Search of Whodunit* (1989) by Werner Holzwarth and Wolf Erlbruch. The book begins with an unidentified animal defecating on Little Mole's head as he peers out of a molehill. What follows is his investigation into which animal did it. Carrying the evidence atop his head, he compares it to the droppings of other animals he meets until he solves the crime. *Mole's Hill* (1994) by Lois Ehlert shows how Mole outwits Fox, Skunk and Raccoon when they threaten to tear through her mound for a path to the pond. Drawing inspiration from a Seneca tale and the flora and fauna local to Wisconsin, Ehlert illustrates the story with her own spin on ribbon appliqué and sewn beadwork, art forms traditional to woodland tribal nations. Consider, too, the protagonist of Dan Yaccarino's picture book *Morris Mole* (2017), who goes on a search for confidence. His difference from other moles, who are big and strong, is a cause of anxiety. When he bucks conformity and digs up instead of down, his life is enriched by what he discovers above ground and he becomes the ambassador to other animals for the moles. This is Plato's allegory of the cave gone right, Morris finding acceptance from his own community for his enlightenment. Here we see moles as autonomous and clever problem-solvers.

The most famous animated mole in the world – and champion trickster of this self-made mole variety – is Krtek, which is Czech

Krtek and builders, Latvia.

for 'Mole'. The creation of animator Zdeněk Miler, Krtek appeared in 45 shorts and six half-hour films between 1957 and 2002, becoming widely beloved on both sides of the Iron Curtain. The story of his inception is fittingly amusing:

In 1954, when what was then Czechoslovakia was under Communist control, [Miler] was working in a movie studio when party bosses commissioned a cartoon to teach children about how trousers are made. The concept was boring, and Mr. Miler did not want to mimic Disney images. Walking in the woods one night, he tripped over a mole's burrow. 'I said, "Here's a good idea,"' he recalled.[52]

Indeed, when giving the cartoons a second thought, the politics of Krtek emerge in a charmingly subversive way. For instance, Miler decided early on that the shorts would be told without dialogue, giving them far more reach than if they would need to be subtitled or dubbed into other languages; as a result, Krtek found 'audiences in more than 80 countries, including China, India and Japan'.[53] Miler, in cutting out speech, freed himself artistically to tell stories that would not be censored; Mickey Mouse, after all, 'was forbidden throughout the Soviet Bloc'.[54] Sociology professor Csaba Szaló notes Krtek is 'an iconic figure . . . [who] is very unique in that he has persevered throughout communist times and after as a kind of persisting cultural figure' in Central and Eastern Europe. When Krtek does vocalize, it is with the giggling of a young child. From freeing a cuckoo from its clock to digging a well in the desert for animals living there and protesting against deforestation to raising an orphaned eagle to maturity, his good-natured exploits attest to a character that is perennially curious and concerned with the welfare of others. If moles could choose a goodwill ambassador to represent them around the world, Krtek

would be the likeliest candidate for the position. He defies every stereotype about moles, standing small but heroically while the human he so often annoys comes away looking the fool.

It is far more common for moles to appear in supporting roles, however, than for them to be the focus. In Brian Jacques' *Redwall* books, a medieval fantasy series for children cast with animals, moles occupy the sidelines. Drawing on his experience as a long-distance lorry driver in Britain, Jacques gave moles 'their own peculiar brand of molespeak, faintly reminiscent of Somerset villagers on the Bristol Channel'.[55] Something about the dialect among the old men he encountered there fitted the way he wished to depict moles in his fantasy world. In his 22-book series, industrious moles, led by a Foremole, come and go. One even preserves ancient scrolls written in molescript, some creative debt here owed to the scribemoles of Horwood's *Duncton Wood*.

Medieval moles also appear in modern-day *Under Wildwood*, the second book of the *Wildwood Chronicles* by Colin Meloy and Carson Ellis. Human protagonist Prue McKeel stumbles upon the subterranean City of Moles and discovers there a dictatorship in need of a coup. Prue and friends assist the mole knights, who are 'equipped with darning needle swords and bottle-cap armor' and led by a salamander-riding leader named High Master Commander Sir Timothy Mole.[56] The moles of Underwood speak in block capitals, Meloy explaining that 'everything is a proclamation to the moles.'[57] In rescuing the Sibyl, a mole prophetess, Prue and friends are given information vital to their adventures and are seen off by the Mole Council. Ellis's delightful art for the book relishes the story, with a map of the Underwood and a skyline of the City of Moles in the conflagration of battle revealing buildings made from cartons, cans, and cardboard boxes with open books for roofs. These moles are mole-sized compared to humans, but they wear outfits, various accoutrements and can grow trailing beards

Krtek merchandise.

in old age. The medieval cultures and finery of Jacques' and Meloy and Ellis's moles suggest there is something acceptably antiquated about moles in the collective imagination. Moles' industrious and seemingly humble lives dovetail nicely with the ways in which we popularly imagine human life during the Dark Ages.

Another light in which moles have been cast teaches children that some individuals are loners. Clara Dillingham Pierson's story 'The Quarrelsome Mole', published in her book *Among the Forest People* (1898), tells of Mr and Mrs Ground Hog's appraisal of a mole moving into the forest. Coming from the meadow, he complains incessantly about how awful his neighbours there were, chiefly Garter Snake, Tree Frog and his fellow moles. He is quickly sized up, based on the first impression he makes, which says rather more about the Ground Hogs than him. Pierson's narration is unrelenting in judgement, too: 'there was not a lonelier or more miserable person than the Mole, who guarded his own rights and told people what he thought of them.'[58] He never gets the chance to show the Ground Hogs what kind of neighbour he is before they condemn him for complaining about his prior neighbours. *The Tale of Grandfather Mole* (1920) by Arthur Scott Bailey is a collection of interconnected animal stories in which Grandfather Mole of Farmer Green's garden plays a central role. Though not mentioned as attired in the book, illustrator Harry L. Smith portrayed him wearing mismatched clothing: striped trousers, suspenders and a bandana. As episodes progress, Grandfather Mole disputes with his worm-eating neighbours, mostly birds, who would love to see him leave the garden, as it would free up resources. In one misadventure, Mrs Wren worries about his grandson Moses wandering the garden. '"Tell me" – Grandfather Mole besought her – "has he a neck?"'[59] He does indeed have a neck, unravelling a case of mistaken identity – it is actually Mr Shrew. In the end, Grandfather Mole is not besmirched by his

Arthur Scott Bailey's Grandfather Mole, drawn by Harry L. Smith, 1920.

Grandfather Mole Made a Rush for Mr. Meadow
Mouse.

neighbours' opinion of him, declaring, 'It's everybody else that's queer – and not I!'[60]

Most charming of all in this genre of bedtime animal stories, Grandfather Frog offers up an explanation for Miner the Mole's underground lifestyle in Thornton W. Burgess's *Mother West Wind 'Why' Stories* (1915). Striped Chipmunk, Johnny Chuck, Jimmy Skunk and Danny Meadow Mouse wonder how 'all their lives Miner the Mole had been one of their nearest neighbors, and yet they didn't know the first thing about him.'[61] Grandfather Frog explains how Miner the Mole's great, great, ever-so-great-grandfather, who lived above ground, never meddled in others' affairs; upon becoming a potential meal for Mr Wolf, Mr Fox and Mr Badger, he dug a tunnel and hid. Realizing he could live safely in solitude in the earth, he remained, 'perfectly happy and satis-fied there, and what is there in life better than to be happy and satisfied?'[62] Miner the Mole, carrying a vocation in his name, does not make an entrance, but his way of life is legitimized by the amphibian sage of the Smiling Pool. Children, especially if they live where molehills are common, are apt to wonder about moles; they are also likely to ponder human neighbours they rarely see. Burgess's presentation of moles *in absentia* is unique in its con-scious refusal to pass judgement on others for keeping to themselves.

The strangest mole trope of all, which is also the predominant mole-related motif in cinema, is that of mole men. A cross between humans and moles and who have their own civilization underground, mole men have never been consistently imagined and their appearance varies from film to film. Typically their mole traits render them strange, but rarely are they outright evil. The earliest examples of mole men portray them as stand-ins for oppressed people who are discriminated against for being different from those in power above ground. This take has shifted towards parody in more recent years, where mole men are monstrous but the humans who fall victim to them are fools deserving of their fate. As such, mole men occupy an idiosyncratic arc in pop culture, going from a misunderstood race deserving of dignity to B-movie fodder, the joke being that it is hard to believe mole men were ever scary to audiences. Tracking how the motif shifted over the past seventy years reveals that film has relegated moles to their usual place in the arts – the periphery – in this case, the outskirts of science fiction, horror and comedy. So why *mole* men instead of some other hybrid? Examining the trope case-by-case offers clues.

In superficial ways, mole men probably derived from the cave-dwelling Morlocks in H. G. Wells's 1895 novel *The Time Machine*. Their cinematic debut came when George Reeves faced a small band of them in the Man of Steel's first feature film, *Superman and the Mole Men* (1951). 'They had the bodies of moles and great big human heads,' Lois Lane explains, 'They were just horrible.'[63] But these 'monsters' are largely victims of misunderstanding. The titular *Mole Men* are played by Johnny Roventini, Billy Curtis, John Bambury and Jerry Maren, all of them middle-aged men of stature somewhere in the range of 1.2 metres (4 ft). Each wears what appear to be heavily pilled onesies with extra hair glued to the backs of their hands and over their eyebrows. They also all sport shine-top male pattern baldness. Audiences anticipating distinctly talpid hybrids are confronted instead by four little men with blandly cautious faces.

Emerging from the deepest oil well ever drilled, two mole men, presumed denizens of a hollow earth environment, spend most of the hour-long movie running about peeping into windows and alarming people just by being different. The nightwatchman at the oil well dies of a heart attack upon seeing them; a girl's mother loses it when she finds them playing ball with her daughter in her

Mole Men lobby card (1951).

bedroom; the whole town, in this pre-Civil Rights Movement American allegory for discrimination, goes torches-and-pitchforks with the aim of killing them. Superman, realizing the mole men are harmless and merely curious about life above ground, flies in to protect them. Cornered atop a dam, one is blasted with a shotgun but Superman catches him before he can contaminate the reservoir – these 1950s mole men are, of course, radioactive. The mob sets dogs on the other mole man, who holes up in a shed. When they set fire to it and he starts pulling up floorboards, one expects he will dig a tunnel to safety. No such luck, however, for the mole man merely crawls out and makes a break for it on foot. The plot comes to a head when the mob threatens to 'string up'

Superman for interfering. He convinces the townspeople to let him negotiate a deal to hand over the injured mole man to his own kind. One hateful townie attempts to ambush the mole men but they blast him in the chest with a ray gun. Superman steps in the way and, being indestructible and of a just heart, winds up escorting the mole men back to the hole they crawled out of at the beginning of the movie. The interactions between mole men and small-town white Americans call to mind the nation's history of lynching African Americans and people of other historically underrepresented groups. Superman, the space alien who passes as a white American, stands in as the conscience for a populace given to attacking those who appear to be different.

Mole men, it turns out, recur in other superhero cartoons and comics. Captain Marvel dealt with them in his comic in February 1944; Underdog fought them in his TV series in 1965. The very first supervillain Marvel's Fantastic Four faced in 1961 was the Mole Man, a former nuclear engineer turned leader of the underground Moloids, a race of subterranean denizens who wear slit-pupil visors and seek war against earth's surface-dwellers. Harvey Elder, reinventing himself as Mole Man, has repeatedly attempted world domination in the decades since his first appearance, from stoking a nuclear war between the USA and Russia to attempting to render all of humankind sightless. Assuredly human, his mole-like features amount to mole stereotypes: nearsightedness, a big nose, a short and stocky frame. He also, naturally, resides beneath the ground. It is interesting to note that the fairy-tale motif of moles as undesirable grooms also occurs in his dealings with She-Hulk, whereby he tricks her into a wedding engagement that flops. We can assume that Elder's self-image as Mole Man is true to heart as, after falling into 'diamond goop' that has the power to 'turn people into what they really are, down deep inside', he is changed into a small, rather helpless mole.[64] In this instance,

Autographed
photo by Mole
Person actor
Robert Herron,
1956.

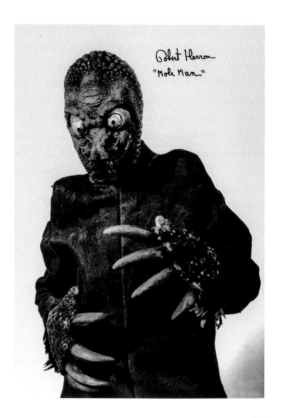

Mole Man's identity as a mole is a metaphor for his own inferiority complex, the curious assumption being that moles must be quite insecure in themselves.

Universal International released its film *The Mole People* to cinemas in 1956. Directed by Virgil W. Vogel, the movie follows archaeologists who fall captive to a relict, underground population of white Sumerians. These archaic people, dressed like elves, are not the mole people. The mole people are a separate humanoid species enslaved by the Sumerians. Tall, hunchbacked and bearing large, clawed hands, they occupy a cavern of mounds where they are whipped into digging. They wear onesies similar to those worn by Superman's mole men, but these are portrayed by actors wearing rubber masks with garish features. More bug-eyed alien than mole, silver compound eyes give these snoutless mole people more of a reptilian look. Their mode of retreat is to slide downward into sand traps, more characteristic of ant-lions than moles. Given their titular status, their lack of screen time is thoroughly disappointing, the story focusing overwhelmingly on the archaeologists. Mole people are a slave class in this underground society: grotesque, disenfranchised, voiceless. If any allegory is meant about the antebellum South, it fails on

Lobby card for *The Mole People* (1956).

the basis of underdevelopment and insensitivity. One of the Sumerians, a young woman named Adad, is Caucasian and ironically considered to have the 'mark of darkness', not white enough for her society. Considered as a fantasy of unconscious attitudes, *The Mole People* unearths American anxieties about racism, the ingrown problem of white supremacy, and the dehumanization of African Americans. The creatures eventually revolt against their masters, a rebellion that fails to rally the audience because it smacks of a mere plot device to aid the archaeologists' escape. The movie was eventually riffed on by the comedy series *Mystery Science Theater 3000*, producing a version arguably more watchable than the original. When Adad is shown watching the slave revolt, Crow T. Robot quips, 'Great, why did I bring democracy to the moles?'[65] Indeed, the movie runs with the myth of 'the white man's burden', rendering its progressive intentions exploitative of the real-world problems it mines.

The Italian movie *Mole Men against the Son of Hercules* (1961) is also questionably racist in its portrayal of mole men, being here a pigmentless people dressed in white capes and with horned, mad-scientist heads of hair who raid villages from underground caverns. Of standard human size and appearance, they are another white-supremacist, industrial order that whips slaves into mining. Their slaves are not creatures, but humans from above ground. It is up to Maciste, as a son of Hercules, and his African friend Bangor to defeat the mole men and their matriarch, bringing peace to those being attacked and enslaved. It comes to pass that, like Adad in *The Mole People*, the queen of the mole men was herself taken from above ground as a child and raised as one of them. Her self-discovery sends her into the sunlight for the first time in her memory, dazzling her so much that she plummets off a cliff to her death. Clearly, these themes are either convergent or lifted from *The Mole People*. The film is notable, however, in that it is

one of the only times an actual mole is seen in a film. Near the end of the first reel, Maciste pulls a live mole right out of the ground by the scruff of its neck. 'Brave little fellow,' he says with a laugh as it struggles in his grip. 'It's a mole,' Bangor says, 'My ancestors ate them.'[66] Maciste lets it go and it burrows into the sand, out of sight, in seconds. Though clumsy in its handling of mole men, the film does go where no other has in terms of showing moviegoers an actual mole.

Mole men later found themselves invoked in subversive music. In 1979, punk band the Dickies put out 'Attack of the Molemen', inspired by and essentially laying out the premise of Universal's film *The Mole People*. The Mole People, an electronic

Mole people emerge from the ground.

tribal house project by Armand Van Helden, later served up minimalist music composed for the rave scene. And in the twenty-first century, the trope of mole men has returned in the service of farce. *Saul of the Mole Men* (2007) was a short-lived TV series spoofing 1970s children's programming, with mole men costumed in the spirit of *H. R. Pufnstuf*. In John Hodgman's book *More Information than You Require* (2008), which poses as an almanac, mole men emerge as 'subterranean *philosophes*, believing in reason, rejecting superstition, and obsessing over building and refining orderly systems – of science, education, government, and especially tunnels'.[67] Hodgman writes of a U.S. census-taker who vanished while accounting for all residents of a mole-man city under Moundsville, West Virginia, producing his 'list of 700 mole men names, sent back to the sunlit lands in 1792, tied to the

Krtek and Max Malwurf (Max Mole), Leipzig, Germany.

152

back of an earwig'.[68] Enthusiastic readers, in the age of social media, responded online with cartoon portraits of each in the 700 Mole-men Project.[69]

In a similarly ridiculous vein, *The Moleman of Belmont Avenue* (2011) is a low-budget comedy written and directed by the actors playing its two main characters. The premise? Two brothers become landlords of an apartment building in Chicago where the residents' pets keep going missing. They discover a mole man lives under the building and, once he starts trying to eat the tenants, they set out to kill him. Unfortunately, the problem is not just one mole man, but an entire group of mole men. However, the brothers discover that running the building's furnace wards them off. This screwball horror comedy amuses, redeemed by cast members like Robert Englund, known best for his turns as Freddy Krueger in the *Nightmare on Elm Street* movies. The mole men are once again beastly: green-blooded, purple-skinned with massive yellow incisors, draped in rags and hobbling at floor level with great, clawed hands. Gone is any intimation at the inhumanity of discrimination or the innate dignity of the mole men. Here they are full-on vermin, likely inspired by stereotypes of the real-life urban 'mole people' living below New York City in the 1980s and '90s.

Rounding out mole men in cinema, consider the mockumentary by Luminoid Films, *The Molers*, an Official Selection of the 2013 Lake Charles Film Festival. This parody of monster-hunting TV series, with a nod to the cult classic sasquatch docudrama *The Legend of Boggy Creek* (1972), delves into what it calls 'Talpidanthropy (n.): Belief in the existence of creatures that are part mole (family *Talpidae*) and part human (*anthropo*, pertaining to man)'.[70] The hour-long movie follows the exploits of Clevis Folger and his cohort, Bip Martin, who claims to have been 'subducted' by mole people. They scour Louisiana ditches and drains for signs of

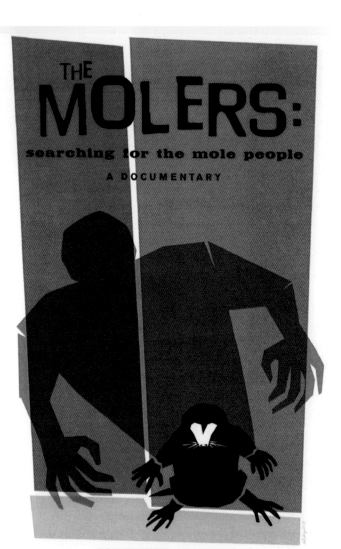

'surfacing', baiting mole people with canned Vienna Sausage and identifying their scat, which is said to petrify in the sun. They also come to the aid of Caroline Clinch Hewitt of Oxfordshire, whose missing husband Bailey has presumably been 'subducted', too. Director James Edmunds plays a charming cameo role as expert Reginald Paste of the fictitious Edith Lowell Danes Center for Cryptozoological Studies at Columbia University. Poking fun at the speculative investigations, the film's way of stopping short of showing viewers a mole person ups its ethos in taking playful jabs at the fringe-theory cottage industry. Mole people, in this instance, are the worry of deluded fools and silly government projects headed by characters with names like General Mellonballer.

The injection of a knowing absurdity in *Molers* and *The Moleman of Belmont Avenue* is a sign that twenty-first-century mole men are not to be pitied. No longer a clumsy, ineffective substitute for oppressed groups of people, the motif of mole men is even more marginalized in the popular imagination today, in which it has succumbed to a mixture of menace and goofiness. Moles are not the typical stuff of nightmares, being small, solitary and not known for attacking people. The mix of man and wolf – the werewolf – carries instantly understood ferocity, given stereotypes about wolves. Moles, however, are thought to be timid, preferring lives of seclusion underground; one would expect that a hybrid race with humans would carry those associations. Occupying separate spheres may have served the motif in the final years of legal segregation in the USA, when the cultural barrier of 'separate but equal' was about to break down: mole men lived underground and humans lived above ground and disruption of this arrangement unsettled many people. But the aspect of real-life moles being a common bane of suburban lawns undermines the dignity earlier film-makers tried to shoehorn into the mole-men trope.

Poster for *The Molers* (2013).

Mole men always want to return below the earth's surface, while the humans always want to find their way back to sunlight. Physiology and resistance to change never give either race a chance to strike a balance in these stories other than reinforced segregation – a theme that could not survive the Civil Rights Movement.

A new, bold take on mole men is the heretofore underrepresented mole *woman*. Los Angeles-based artist Vanessa Terrell Key's sculpture *Queenie of the Hill* offers a concept long overdue, the motif having consistently left women out for seventy years. Similar to the hybrid-human sculptures of Patricia Piccinni, Key's *Queenie* is a hyper-realistic crossing of star-nosed mole and woman, wrought in airbrushed and hand-painted polymer clay, resin, glass and epoxy. Furless and nude, she rises from a molehill with quiet power, beautiful in her defiance of beauty norms; as Key explained to me, 'She's self-confident regardless of what others may think of her appearance.' Her Eimer's organs are exquisitely rendered and the ease in her skyward gaze suggests she is as comfortable above ground as she is below it. Why it has taken so long for a mole woman to rise up in our awareness when mole men have enjoyed so many permutations for decades is a strange blind spot in the mole-men motif. Queenie is a welcome corrective, toppling the trope's gendered one-sidedness.

If anything, all of the preceding examples of moles appearing throughout popular culture, from distant Elizabethan theatre to recent electronic media, prove that they are as adaptable and at home in the peripheries of artistic expression as they are just under the surface of our lawns. Rarely taking the lead, their presence at the outskirts of stories mirrors their presence in people's lives. In some ways, a 1958 song by the Southlanders, 'The Mole in the Hole', perfectly illustrates the place of moles in pop culture and literature. The comic tune gives an echoing voice to its subject, with bass singer Harry Wilmot revealing that he is a mole

and he lives in a hole. Failing to make the charts, the pop song nevertheless became an essential part of the group's performances throughout their career. So it goes with the mole in the arts: the animal has certainly received highly focused, even loving attention from some of the finest artists – though often not – and either way has ended up represented on the edges of human imagination, finding there both affection and disregard.

Mole mascot for an optometrist, Elberfeld, Germany.

7 The Hunted Mole

'A neighbour saw what you were doing,' they explained, 'and thought you were trying to commit suicide.'

Two police officers, conducting a welfare check on a woman in Des Moines, Iowa, had found her doing a bit of gardening. In the driveway her car was parked but left running, a length of garden hose attached to its exhaust pipe with its other end trailing into a hole in the ground. The police officers had pulled up in their car, leapt out, and then eased upon taking in the details of the scene and finding her well. When they asked her what she was doing, she dreaded they were about to tell her she was killing an endangered species and subject to a massive fine.

'I'm trying to get rid of moles,' she told them. Convinced by now that she posed no threat to herself, the officers were pleasantly chatty, wanting to know how it was going. There was no triumph to share. She was losing the war.

I interviewed the aggrieved agronomist about her experiences with moles in her garden on a tip from my dad that she had a mole story to tell. It all occurred twenty years ago, a summer-long struggle to reclaim her lawn in a quiet, wooded residential neighbourhood. The first real sign of trouble was an unevenness in the front and back gardens, that made mowing a topsy-turvy affair. Over several years, it became clear that this was not due to the earth settling; rather, it was the work of something settling in the earth. When the grass started dying off, she took her problem at home to a colleague working in wildlife biology. He was the one to tell her she had moles.

'How do I get rid of them?' she asked.

'Well,' he said, 'you don't.'

Undeterred, she started reading up on old wives' tales of how to eradicate them. Somewhere she read moles ate grubs, and she set to pickling her grass with pesticide. The moles persisted. She set mousetraps with peanut butter at a tunnel entrance, to no avail. She did catch one, after digging out a tunnel and setting a live trap there. It died before she found it. Seeing how small the mole was, it surprised her how effective it was at killing off her lawn. Then she read that carbon monoxide pumped into their tunnels would put them to sleep. 'I should've known better,' she reflects, 'I'm a soil scientist.' That is, she knew the ground is porous and the deadly gas would not traipse neatly through the tunnel system, filling all of its chambers. What she did not know is that the method is unlikely to kill moles because of their inherent

A surfeit of molehills.

Exposed mole tunnels, showing damage to land.

biological advantages when it comes to living in conditions with minimal amounts of oxygen.

The guide suggested using a hose attached to the exhaust port on a gas-powered lawnmower. Snaking the hose down a tunnel entrance and letting the lawnmower run was the idea. But her lawnmower did not have an exhaust port where she could affix the hose. She turned then to her car, which led to neighbourly concern, which led to emergency services rushing to her home.

The method, it turns out, did not rid her property of moles. The garden worsened and she eventually took to levelling it with a core aerator, a labour-intensive job requiring a lot of hard work before reseeding. Sometime later, she bumped into the colleague who had given her advice on the issue. He asked, 'Did you ever solve the mole problem?'

'Why, yes,' she told him. 'I moved!'

Indeed, homeowners have been known to go to astonishing ends in attempting to rid their gardens of moles. A popular modern American approach with absolutely no proof of success is to drop a stick of Wrigley's Juicy Fruit chewing gum into a mole hole. The folk belief is that they love the brand's taste and eating it 'gums up' their digestive tract and constipates them to death. Another hare-brained method that does nothing to deter moles is the practice of burying empty bottles with the neck open at ground level. The idea here is that as wind blows across the mouths of the bottles, playing them like flutes, the sound waves will reverberate through the earth and annoy the moles into vacating the premises. Again, this does not work. Along the same line, however, there are sonic devices on the market advertised as driving moles away with pulses of subterranean sound. Those vouching for these methods, maintaining that the mole or moles left their property, are likely correct about an eventuality while being wrong about the cause. Moles, while territorial, are not beholden to a single tunnel system and will leave one for another for any number of reasons, especially if food has gone scarce. In addition to this, once a tunnel system is built, it can stand for untold generations. Real estate, from the perspective of moles, oftentimes consists of reclaiming a fixer-upper and, when bored of the project, flipping it.

'Take a turn in the morning round the garden or meadow where you wish to destroy the moles; they are then at work.'[1] So begins a guide to mole-hunting for the average Joe, translated from French into English and published in Edinburgh in 1791. Its unattributed author proffers five extirpation methods: (1) if the mole happens to be kicking up a mound and you happen to be present for it, dig it out with a spade; (2) clear a molehill, pour a bottle of water down the hole, catch the mole by hand as it tries to escape from drowning; (3) if it happens to be digging a surface run, stomp behind it to collapse the tunnel, dig it out; (4) (deemed 'the most common' case)[2] expose 36–43 centimetres (15 to 18 in.)

of a mole's tunnel while it is kicking up a hill, wait for it to return to the now-exposed tunnel, block its escape with a spade, wait for it to dig straight down, pour water in, grab it when it comes up; (5) when there are three or more molehills and the mole's whereabouts are unknown, pretty much repeat the fourth method with

John Vine, the
celebrated Kentish
and Surrey
Molecatcher,
1804.

the addition of patience in waiting for the mole to make itself
known at one end or the other of the exposed track. 'These are all
the varieties of cases that can occur,'[3] the author claims, and yet
all of it seems impractical, slipshod and dependent upon easily
missed opportunity. Even those desperate to rid their patch of

green of moles are likely to reject the time and effort required to evict an interloper – not to mention the problem of what to do with the moles once caught.

Enter the mole-catchers: professionals whose livelihood is made by eradicating moles. Given the endangered natures of golden moles and marsupial moles, neither is legally hunted. The talpids, however, are. In North America, many people working in pest control include moles among the animals they will dispatch, but across Europe the role has largely been handled exclusively by specialists. Digging into their past, journalist Brendan Borrell found that 'in the 18th century mole-catchers were employed by every parish in England to keep the mole population under control. Catching these creatures required such skill that practitioners were remunerated more generously than surgeons.'[4] These individuals could make a living wage in part because their expert knowledge was fiercely guarded. Moles present such a unique ecology that typical methods of trapping employed with other pest species simply would not work on them. As such, those who have traditionally known the most about moles are the people who work to kill them, a bizarre dynamic of understanding that is only just beginning to be eclipsed by those studying them in the sciences. Says mole-catcher Jeff Nicholls,

in order to fully appreciate the mole you will need to feel respect towards the velvet-coated little creature, and to understand the knowledge that has passed from mole to man, in one of the strangest relationships that has led so many others to be a mole catcher.[5]

The Ribblesdale Mole-catcher, 19th-century Yorkshire.

Today's hotbed for the practice of traditional mole-catching is Britain. Estimates put 'the entire mole population in Great Britain . . . at 31 million',[6] a number that fluctuates substantially

164

The Ribblesdale "Mole Catcher"

throughout the year as litters are reared and thinned out through natural causes. Mole-catching barely puts a dent in the population.

To help me better understand the job, Norfolk's very own Lady Mole Catcher®, Louise Chapman, let me shadow her as she made her usual rounds on 30 May 2017. She begins each day in Norwich but her travels from site to site take her all over the county. Her mole-catching-mobile, an Audi A3, is decorated with symbols advertising the British Mole Catchers Register and her Lady Mole

Llanboidy Mole Catcher by James Lewis Walters, 1900, oil on canvas.

Catcher® trademark. The best portion of the day I spent with her involved getting from this place to that place, and her primary duty was inspecting traps she had already set. Clients she visited ranged from homeowners to a primary school, a home for people with disabilities and even the marina. Some were at home and greeted her with waves from windows when she arrived with bucket full of traps and Buddy, her mild-mannered Jack Russell. 'He's scared of them,' she laughs when I ask if he assists in catching moles. Her route is determined by her current list of trap locations and where they exist in relation to one another; without plotting a deliberate route, her day could easily take twice as long to complete. Also essential for the job: coffee. The baristas of Norwich know Chapman and Buddy well, adding some regular interaction to what is often a solitary business.

Her day is punctuated by calls from potential clients. The care-taker for the primary school rang her the evening before, so that was her first stop. Three rather fresh hills lurked along the edge of the playing field. The caretaker and I gawked as Chapman went about her mysterious work laying a trap. Later, having set up her mole-catcher mobile for hands-free calls, a woman called with an inquiry: 'We've just this morning discovered some friends at the bottom of the garden. Could you come round and have a look?' Recalibrating her route, Chapman drove straight over to the woman's house and met her in the driveway. We were led straight away into the back garden where, amid the incongruous surprise of three tortoises munching on lettuce, two sizable discs of flattened earth spotted the grass. The woman's husband, having found molehills at dawn, had stomped them flat – an interference most people do not realize can compromise a clean catch. Chapman explained it is a common occurrence as well as an understand-able one; the instinct to put back what has been kicked up, while relatable, can tip off the mole that he or she is meeting resistance and should be cautious. In such cases, Chapman has to tell the potential client to call again if fresh hills arise – and to please refrain from levelling them if they do.

The day I spent with her – broken up by a manicure appointment, as she doesn't let mole-catching pose an injunction against having nice nails – Chapman caught three moles: one at the home for disabled people and two at the residence of the superintendent of police, one of which was caught in his front garden and one in the back, both with tunnel traps. I was surprised to witness how clean they were when pulled from the earth. She quietly showed me the strong forepaws, as if prepared to read its palms – which were, again, surprisingly spotless – and gently nudged the second 'thumb', a wee flap on the side that helps in scooping dirt. The reality of mole-catching is that they are caught dead, making it a job ill-suited to the squeamish. Live moles, quite apart from being distressed at being handled, are aggressively territorial, meaning that release at another site would likely lead to a fight to the death with the resident mole. When Chapman finds a sprung trap, she prefers to pull it out in front of the customer. If he or she is not home, she will snap a photo of it with her smartphone and send it to the client. As she puts it, 'People do like to see a body.'[7] Some mole-catchers, she warned me, are dishonest. Some have been known to carry dead moles on their person; upon visiting a property for the third or fourth time, and determining a mole has abandoned the site, a mendacious mole-catcher will produce the dead mole from his or her pocket as one caught there, collecting an unearned bounty.

Most of the potential ways to catch moles employ kill-traps. While there do exist cylindrical live traps on the market, many complain they are inhumane because, given moles' high metabolisms and need to eat often, many will die in them from anxiety, starvation or hypothermia if they are not checked every four hours. The preferred means point to setting traps in their tunnels that can be checked later. Historically, the Romans set drop traps using clay pots filled with water and buried to drown multiple moles. Nicholls explains, 'They were operated by a trap door in a piece of wood laid across the top, which the mole fell through when the pot had been successfully placed in a main tunnel.'[8] A far more elaborate trap of old, which inspired the design of metal traps in use today, was the snare. This trap consists of a rectangular wooden or clay tile with holes at each corner. Through these were looped snares of braided horsehair set slack to a 'mumble pin' at the centre of the tile – the pin so named because in setting the snare a mole-catcher would hold it in his mouth and 'would have had to mumble, if he'd had to talk to anyone'.[9] This device was set into the top of a dug-out mole tunnel and covered over so only the main strand of plaited horsehair rose from the earth. The mole-catcher would then lodge a stick of willow close by, bend it towards the buried trap and tie the horsehair tightly to it. When the bender stick bobbed, indicating a mole had triggered the

New Trap for catching Moles.   299

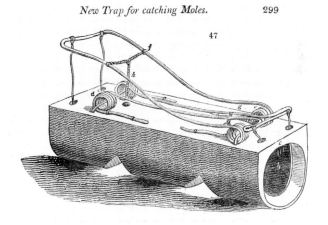

Nineteenth-century design for a tunnel trap, from *The Gardener's Magazine and Register of Rural and Domestic Improvement*, 1826.

mumble pin and was caught in the loops of hair, the mole-catcher pulled it out and killed his prey. According to Nicholls, 'The use of snares in this way was the main method of catching moles for hundreds of years.'[10]

Today there are three kinds of metal traps used in the UK by mole-catchers: the scissor trap, the tunnel or half-barrel Duffus trap and the Talpex trap. All are set at ground level in surface

'Les Taupes' by Felix Bracquemond, 1854.

runs, where the least amount of disturbance needs be made to a mole's tunnel system. The scissor trap, often powered by a flat spring, has two pairs of trap jaws that are set off by a mumble pin; despite being called a scissor trap, the jaws are not sharpened. When brought together by an unwitting mole, they crush its top ribs behind its forelimbs in a killing stroke. The width of this trap makes it a good choice for a tight fit. The tunnel trap, also known as the half-barrel or Duffus trap, calls for a longer, straighter stretch of a mole's surface run. Scottish shepherd and mole-catcher John Duffus, inspired by the traps already in use, invented his own in 1923; 'patent no. 203,484, which was the final design, . . . is still the half-barrel trap we see today.'[11] The trap body is a curved section of sheet metal that caps the exposed tunnel like a tin roof. Under it are mumble pins triggering wire trap loops, which are powered by springs up top. Worries that there was not enough force in the trap to ensure a humane death blow led to modifications in the shape of the loops and strength of the mechanism. The mole, wandering in from either tunnel direction, steps through the loop, trips the spring and has its chest crushed as it is pulled taut against the metal ceiling. The Talpex trap is a gripper in the vein of the scissor, but its force is stronger. It requires more space in a tunnel than other traps when set but makes use of the inevitability of disturbing the soil. The mole-catcher will fill loose dirt around the trap once set; when the mole comes back through and sets to clearing what looks like a cave-in, the trap's plate is tripped. Its coil spring then crushes the mole's upper body with 7 kilograms (70 N) of force.

The plunger trap is also used in the United States, though banned in the European Union for being inhumane. It consists of a spring-loaded trigger that, when tripped, sends six harpoons straight down into the tunnel, impaling the mole. A similar trap, marketed as the Anglo Impassable, was used in Britain at the turn of the twentieth century, but its method of piercing the hide ruined any chances of selling the fur. Another once-common method of mole control is the use of strychnine; the poison was banned across the UK in 2006 for its inhumane effects. Strychnine, an alkaloid highly toxic to all vertebrates, renders a definite but horrific death, inflicting suffocating convulsions to the end. Gorman and Stone share that 25 strychnine-poisoned worms could kill an entire hectare (2.5 acres) of moles but, since the poison fouls the flavour of worms, devious means were required to achieve that efficiency: 'Many experienced mole poisoners adopt a more subtle approach and prefer to soak a cotton thread in a solution of strychnine and then to thread it through the centre of a worm with the aid of a darning needle.'[12] A 2016 study found that the projected explosion in the mole population following the strychnine ban never precipitated. It also noted that 'Moles have been treated unequally to most other species in wildlife management, with a lower welfare threshold tolerated as evidenced by the use of strychnine and unregulated traps.'[13]

And yet Nicholls stresses the necessity of trapping that delivers a swift kill so that the mole suffers as little as possible: 'The need to supply the highest level of welfare towards the target mole at all times is the difference between those who merit the title of mole catcher, and those who do not.'[14] Chapman iterates the same ethic about the job. For professionals, every situation is different and must be assessed by its own features. 'Basically,' Chapman told me, 'I read the ground.' This includes taking in where the mole has dug tunnels leading to and from its refuse heaps. Molehills are essentially tunnel plugs, making them poor sites to lay a trap; mole-catchers always seek out an undisturbed stretch of underground pathway to lay their traps. A cane-sized rod with a handle on one end and a metal bulb on the other – called a mole probe – is used to find such a tunnel. One knows a tunnel is there when

Mole-catcher in *American Homes and Gardens* (1905).

meeting no resistance in plunging the probe into the earth. Using a garden spade, the mole-catcher cuts out a circle of turf above, breaking open a little window on the smooth tunnel.

Plenty of obstacles must be addressed for a clean catch, from the detectable twists and turns of a run to the moisture and type of soil. One of the most frustrating occurrences is the presence of stony soil. 'Stones get in the way,' Chapman explained, as she let me reach in and feel a rock obstructing a good portion of a surface run. If it will not cause much disruption, the stone can simply be removed; if the soil is soft enough, the stone can simply be pressed into the tunnel wall (the mole probe can be used for leverage in poking an intrusive rock into the earth). Once clear, Chapman determines which of the three traps to use, sets the appropriate one, and covers the top to block out light. 'Tight and tidy,' as she puts it. The tops of the traps are designed to be left to the open air so that one can tell at a glance if they have sprung. She marks each with a small orange flag and goes on her way. Quite typically, she

will only set one trap at a site. 'That's the skill,' she says, 'one mole, one trap.'

But moles are clever when it comes to distrusting changes in their tunnels they did not make themselves. It is not uncommon to pull out a sprung trap and find it clogged with dirt; if moles detect a trap, they will backfill it, setting it off and abandoning the stretch of tunnel on the other side. This behaviour likely contributes to the respect mole-catchers develop for moles, for the creatures exhibit an intelligence not unlike their own in their efforts to trap them. The garden of one of Chapman's clients possessed just such a mole. I accompanied her on her third visit to check four traps. There were two fresh hills but one of the traps, a Duffus half-barrel, had sprung. When she pulled it up, a solid cylinder of soil came up with it. This mole, in all his or her wisdom, was also burrowing alongside a patio, flush with its edge, which can make trap-setting particularly difficult. In mole-catching lingo, the mole had gone 'trap-shy'. 'You're trying to outwit fascinating, clever animals,' she reiterates, 'It takes knowledge and respect.'[15] If the mole evades capture or, more typically, abandons

Louise Chapman, Norfolk's very own Lady Mole Catcher®, and Buddy, May 2017.

the tunnel system for another somewhere else, the mole-catcher does not get paid. 'No mole, no fee' is mole-catchers' industry-wide motto.

Chapman's work is not limited to her activities as Norfolk's very own Lady Mole Catcher®. She also heads up the British Mole Catchers Register (BMCR) and delivers talks on mole-catching to groups year-round. The BMCR is an organization linking Britons seeking the services of traditional mole-catchers while educating the public about the craft of traditional mole-catching. All of this is the culmination of Chapman's experiences. Graduating from university with an honours degree in English, she taught English and drama to secondary school students before following her desire to find a job where she could be on the move and outdoors every day. Apprenticed to mole-catcher John Lill in 2010, she soon bounded to the forefront of traditional mole-catching. Energetic, with a live-wire personality and a hearty sense of humour, she and her timorous terrier Buddy capsize stereotypes of those working in pest control. John Clare's 1835 poem 'The Mole-catcher' epitomizes what people expect of one: 'Tattered and ragg'd, with greatcoat tied in strings, / And collared up to keep his chin from cold, / The old mole-catcher on his journey sings.'[16] Clare depicts the stereotypical mole-catcher accompanied by a 'shaggy dog infirm and old'[17] and casts him as a killer who cheats: 'With stick and spud he tries the new-made hills / And bears his cheating traps from place to place; / Full many are the miners that he kills.'[18] Historically and presently, mole-catching is a male-dominated field; in 2015, of the roughly one hundred traditional mole-catchers in Britain, 'only six of those registered by [the BMCR were] women.'[19] Chapman maintains a presence across social media platforms, sharing facts about moles but also passing on seasonal changes in the landscape that she notices while going about her business. When I met her, she even offered me a fridge magnet with her logo and contact number. As such, she has emerged as someone figuring out how to market an ancient trade in the twenty-first century.

'She's an embarrassment to proper professional mole catchers,' according to Ann Chippendale.[20] A Lancashire-based mole-catcher, Chippendale started an organization to rival the BMCR: the Association of Professional Mole Catchers. A third body, the non-profit Guild of British Molecatchers, also exists and offers an On-line Accreditation Academy. Most of the bad blood seems to come down to business competition that is perhaps aggravated by the industry being so small. Borrell notes, 'The world of mole catching is bitterly divided between those who believe that traps

A 19th-century French *taupier* (mole-catcher).

should be checked every 24 hours – to ensure that any injured moles are dispatched quickly, rather than being left to die a slow and agonizing death – and those who don't.'[21] Chapman checks her own traps as often as she can, but making rounds of Norfolk alone typically means driving up to 800 kilometres (500 mi.) per week. When meeting with clients, she tells them to contact her immediately if they notice one of the traps has sprung, speaking to her experience as an educator. Other mole-catchers – like Nicholls, who redesigned the Duffus with a stronger kill-spring in 2008 – have actively campaigned for a legal requirement to check traps once every 24 hours.

Still others, such as zoologist Rob Atkinson, would like to see mole-catching banned across the board. One place where moles are fully protected from the hunt by permit restrictions is Germany. This sort of reform seems unlikely in Britain, whose

Mole carcasses, Bowland, Lancashire, England, 2008.

own King William III, also known as William of Orange, died from complications after a horse-riding accident near Hampton Court that resulted from his steed, Sorrel, tripping on a molehill. Say Gorman and Stone, 'Jacobites everywhere were delighted, and henceforth drank a toast to "the little gentleman in the black velvet waistcoat".'[22] Indeed, moles have a capacity like none other to dismay landscapers in charge of golf courses and football pitches, blotting the green with their mounds but also miring it with an increased risk for turned ankles. Farmers who graze livestock will argue the soil from molehills spoils silage fed to their animals in winter months, causing illness or even death. Those upset by the animal's uncanny ability to disrupt their efforts at manicuring a garden seem unlikely to warm to the mole any time soon. 'I meet people who are traumatized by the damage to their gardens,' says Chapman. 'They go away on holiday and come back a fortnight later to a scene from the Somme. It can send them a little bit mad.'[23] Indeed, people living across North America and in Japan also trap moles, though zeal for the practice seems strongest in Britain.

As mentioned with regard to Graham Mort's poem 'Mole Totem', mole-catchers in rural parts of Britain and Europe still display carcasses, hung by nose or tail, in rows along landowners' fences, a sight hard to forget once encountered. Professional mole-catchers have it that the practice is traditional and allows them to prove to a farmer how many moles were caught, in order to receive proper payment; not taking them down prevents anyone from hanging them from another farmer's fence and being paid twice. In the era of social media, people have shared their alarm at the macabre sight with 'likes' and retweets, such as when Sally Lyons let it be known that she found fifty dead moles strung along a fence on Denbigh Moors in January 2015. The Royal Society for the Prevention of Cruelty to Animals (RSPCA), refusing to intervene, released a statement: 'We sympathise that finding dead animals in such circumstances can be distressing but our inspectorate exists to investigate and tackle cruelty and the RSPCA will only become involved if there appear to be any offences committed.'[24] Chapman does not employ the method, typically dispatching suburban moles a few at a time. Sometimes she reburies the dead moles in their tunnels, others she leaves in a hedgerow for a fox or badger to find.

The day spent with Chapman was a memorable one, with some notably thought-provoking moments. At one property sporting its own pond, she pointed out a molehill a fox had sullied with droppings. Something in the competitive marking of territory made immediate sense; the one-upmanship of a fox so rudely sticking it to a mole also called to mind the Ainu myth of the mole burning the demon to ashes from which arose cats and foxes. This fox's scat spoke to an ancient back-and-forth between the species. Moles, while keeping to themselves, do exist in relation to other creatures and the goings-on of their environments. Chapman's understanding of the mole also made itself known in her considerations of its lot in life. The year 2017 saw a dry spring in Norfolk and much of England, which sent moles deeper underground because their prey – worms – follow moisture down. In dry conditions, it is hard to set a trap because it is hard to predict where a mole will go. 'With no rain, it's hard for the mole, too,' she told me, exhibiting the empathy mole-catchers deem crucial for any kind of ongoing success in their trade.

For those looking to unleash their frustration about the mounds in their gardens without bringing death to their makers, an alternative might be found in the local arcade – though it will do nothing for one's lawn. Whac-A-Mole is a classic arcade game that is something of a missing link between carnival and video games. The player, wielding a padded mallet, stands before a cabinet with five holes across the top. When a likeness of a mole pops up, the player bops it to accrue points. As the game goes on, the moles spring up and hide again, whether or not the player is quick enough for them. Hand–eye coordination, agility and speed are required to rack up a good score. The game's title has entered the popular lexicon, the *OED* defining the use of 'whack-a-mole' as referencing 'a problem which is addressed in a piecemeal or superficial manner, resulting merely in temporary, minor, or localized improvement, or to a situation in which problems continually or unpredictably arise'. The game has become a metaphor for everything from solid-state drives in computing to counter-insurgency in the 'War on Terror' and the all-too-typical rigours of parenting. 'Family life in our time sometimes seems like game of Whac-a-Mole,' explains the narrator of a George Saunders short story.

Whac-A-Mole at the Oregon State Fair.

Plastic mole emerges, you whack with hammer, he dies,
falls, another emerges, you whack, kill? Sometimes seems
that, as soon as one kid happy, another kid 'pops up',
i.e., registers complaint, requiring parent to 'whack' kid,
i.e. address complaint.[25]

A creation of the 1970s, Whac-A-Mole's origins are as elusive as
the model for its design. An American manufacturer called Bob's
Space Racers claims the earliest make in 1971, but this is difficult
to verify.[26] Between 1974 and 1975, Japanese designer Kazuo
Yoshida conceived of and tweaked a game licensed to Bandai in
1977 as モグラ退治 (Mole Buster), which is essentially the
same, though his early targets were mock-ups of politicians.[27]
In that window of time, an American entrepreneur who saw the
Japanese prototype on the trade floor at the International
Association of Amusement Parks and Attractions (IAAPA) convention hired animatronics wunderkind Aaron Fechter to invent
a similar game based on his description. Fechter does not recall

how moles (as opposed to, say, gophers) were settled upon, but told me, 'the name, "Whac-a-Mole", hit me as a play on the word "guacamole".'[28] The technology he used – pneumatics with electronic controls triggered by tones on a tape – could stand up to excessive beatings in multiplayer cabinets. This version, released in 1976, became the most popular Whac-A-Mole on the market.

The game is historically significant for numerous reasons. Psychologists Luca Chittaro and Riccardo Sioni, who study violence in video games, assert, 'The classic Whac-A-Mole arcade game is the first example of a popular genre (Whac-A-Mole games) in which a specific violent element (i.e., aggression towards non-human animal species) seems to be central to the user experience.'[29] They note that the common perception of moles being a nuisance and a pest may be part of people's willingness to take enthusiastically to the game. It might be easier – even conscience-free – to kill an imitation mole than it is to kill a virtual person.

Mole carcasses hung along fence, Lambley, England, 2017.

A reason for the success of Whac-A-Mole games might thus be that they allow players to engage in violent acts against species that do not elicit the negative physiological responses (and affect) that the literature has instead highlighted for acts of killing or wounding virtual human beings.[30]

On this count, Fechter is repentant. In 2015, at the IAAPA convention where his relationship with Whac-A-Mole began, he unveiled Bashy Bug, a new arcade game where the player uses a flip-flop to smack a giant cockroach dashing back and forth. '[Bashy Bug] is my apology for creating a game, in my less mature days, of violence against an innocent mammal who does not deserve the aggression,' Fechter confided to me. 'In my new game, we will be whacking post-apocalyptic cockroaches, who actually deserve to die.'[31]

In twenty-first-century Britain, badgers have found advocates in activist organizations such as Stop the Cull, who oppose the regular farming practice of culling badgers, believing it is inhumane. No such movement has yet formed in the interest of protecting moles, though public opinion could shift in that direction. 'Don't moles have a right to life too?' asks Patrick Barkham in *The Guardian*.[32] Mark Cocker of Claxton, Norfolk, reports simply shovelling molehills from his lawn to his vegetable-growing patch. He, too, asks, 'is the killing really necessary?'[33] Those preferring a pristine garden or undisturbed grazing for their livestock seem to think so. So long as moles straddle the line in people's estimations between wildlife and vermin, the tradition of mole-catching is sure to continue.

Epilogue: Making Mountains out of Molehills

The most popular brand of sparkling mineral water in Mexico since 1895, which has also found great popularity in Texas, is called Topo Chico. Bottled near Monterrey, Mexico, it is named for the Cerro del Topo Chico (Hill of the Mole Boy). More mountain than hill, the springs from which Topo Chico is bottled can be found at its base. The sparkling mineral water's bottler makes no mention of mole boys or molehills in its 'Legend of Topo Chico', promoting a story of Aztec Emperor Moctezuma I's daughter being healed by the spring water. Many American consumers are likely oblivious to the mole-ishness of what they are drinking. And Cerro del Topo Chico may be the only revered molehill on the planet, given that the little heaps of soil so typically inspire everything from annoyance to dismay – even outrage.

'Don't make a mountain out of a molehill,' we say, advising others, or even ourselves, to put a problem into perspective. The *OED* traces its earliest recorded use to John Foxe's *Ecclesiasticall History Contaynyng the Actes and Munumentes of Thynges Passed* in 1570: 'To much amplifying thinges yt be but small, makyng mountaines of Molehils'. This idiom of diminishment discourages overreaction. It casts the molehill, kicked up by an industrious little insectivore, as inconsequential, something that must not be fixated upon as a dire hurdle in our lives. And really, that is where the mole seems to stand in most people's consciousness

today. As pests go, they are not the worst. As curiosities, their elusive, subterranean existence makes direct encounters with people few and far between. Yet the lives they lead, the adaptations they have accrued and their understated place in the stories we tell all reveal a solitary animal perfectly at home just out of sight in conditions most of us do not bother to fathom and could never tolerate if subjected to them. We may not understand what sent their ancestors underground to begin with but, whether these hard-working, exceedingly sensitive creatures vex us or raise our sympathies, moles seem fated to be neighbours we will never know all that well.

Timeline of the Mole

57–50 million BC	37 million BC	34 million BC	22 million BC
The ancestor species of African golden moles splits from the order *Insectivora*	The burrowing *Eotalpa* has evolved, a direct ancestor of today's talpid moles in Europe, Asia and North America	*Oreotalpa florissantensis* living in what is now North America, marking a split between Old World and New World moles	Ancestors of the marsupial mole have evolved in the prehistoric rainforests of Australia

1702		c. 1900	1908
King William III of England is thrown and injured when his horse, Sorrel, trips on a molehill; he dies soon after		Queen Alexandra popularizes moleskin as a high-society garment material to curb a perceived overpopulation of moles in Wales	Kenneth Grahame publishes *The Wind in the Willows*, introducing readers to Mole

1968		1974	1976
Americans build and defend Patrol Base Mole City during the Vietnam War		John le Carré uses the word 'mole' to describe a spy entrenched in another country's intelligence agency, in the novel *Tinker Tailor Soldier Spy*	Whac-A-Mole arcade game becomes a worldwide amusements sensation

6 million BC	5.6 million–1.3 million BC	1st–4th century AD	1566
Ancestors of Old World moles split between Eurasia and Asia	Ancestors of Japanese moles make four migrations into Japan via an open route across the Korean Strait	Romans use buried clay pots to trap and drown moles	Mole-catching becomes national paid bounty-hunting in England with Elizabeth I's government's Act for the Preservation of Grain

1923	1950s	1956	1957
Mole-catcher John Duffus patents the metal half-barrel tunnel trap	Gillian Godfrey is the first scientist to track moles underground, using a radioactive isotope affixed to their tails and a Geiger counter	Universal Pictures releases the science fiction film *The Mole People*	Czech animator Zdeněk Miler brings out the first Krtek cartoon

1980	1984	2005	2006
William Horwood's epic fantasy series about moles begins with publication of *Duncton Wood*	*Wanted: Monty Mole* debuts as the first computer game whose main character is a mole	Guinness World Records honours the star-nosed mole as the fastest eater among mammals	Strychnine poisoning banned in the UK, sparking renewed interest in traditional techniques of mole-catching

References

FOREWORD

1 Elon Gilad, 'Word of the Day / Khafarperet: The Word that Means Mole but Shouldn't', www.haaretz.com, 29 April 2014.
2 Aristotle, *Metaphysics*, book 5, www.perseus.tufts.edu, accessed 13 April 2018.

1 EVOLUTION

1 Stephen Jay Gould, *The Structure of Evolutionary Theory* (London and Cambridge, MA, 2002), p. 262.
2 William Paley, *Natural Theology*, 5th edn (London, 1803), p. 294.
3 Ibid., p. 296.
4 Charles Darwin, *The Illustrated Origin of Species*, ed. Richard E. Leakey (London and Boston, MA, 1979), p. 96.
5 Ibid., p. 208.
6 H. W. Shimer, 'Adaptations to Aquatic, Arboreal, Fossorial and Cursorial Habits in Mammals. III. Fossorial Adaptations', *American Naturalist*, XXXVII/444 (December 1903), pp. 824–5.
7 Jerry J. Hooker, 'Skeletal Adaptations and Phylogeny of the Oldest Mole *Eotalpa* (Talpidae, Lipotyphla, Mammalia) from the UK Eocene: The Beginning of Fossoriality in Moles', *Palaeontology*, LIX/2 (2016), p. 195.
8 Howard P. Whidden, 'Comparative Myology of Moles and the Phylogeny of the Talpidae (Mammalia, Lipotyphla)', *American Museum Novitates*, 3294 (25 April 2000), p. 50.

9 Anna Loy et al., 'Origin and Evolution of Western European Moles (Genus *Talpa*, Insectivora): A Multidisciplinary Approach', *Mammal Study*, XXX/1 (2005), p. S14.

10 Ibid., p. S15.

11 Karen J. Lloyd and Jaelyn J. Eberle, 'A New Talpid from the Late Eocene of North America', *Acta Palaeontologica Polonica*, LIII/3 (2008), p. 542.

12 Akio Shinohara et al., 'Evolution and Biogeography of Talpid Moles from Continental East Asia and the Japanese Islands Inferred from Mitochondrial and Nuclear Gene Sequences', *Zoological Science*, XXI/12 (2004), p. 1183.

13 Shin-ichiro Kawada et al., 'Karyological Study of the Malaysian Mole, *Euroscaptor micrura malayana* (Insectivora, Talpidae) from Cameron Highlands, Peninsular Malaysia', *Mammal Study*, XXX/2 (2005), p. 114.

14 Akio Shinohara, Kevin Campbell and Hitoshi Suzuki, 'An Evolutionary View on the Japanese Talpids Based on Nucleotide Sequences', *Mammal Study*, XXX (2005), p. S23.

15 Takashi Kirihara et al., 'Spatial and Temporal Aspects of Occurrence of *Mogera* Species in the Japanese Islands Inferred from Mitochondrial and Nuclear Gene Sequences', *Zoological Science*, XXX/4 (2013), p. 279.

16 Yasushi Yokohata, 'A Brief Review of the Biology on Moles in Japan', *Mammal Study*, XXX (2005), p. S27.

17 Achim H. Schwermann and Richard S. Thompson, 'Extraordinarily Preserved Talpids (Mammalia, Lipotyphla) and the Evolution of Fossoriality', *Journal of Vertebrate Paleontology*, XXXV/4 (2015), p. 20.

18 Quoted in Julia Franz, 'The Star-nosed Mole Takes Adaptation to the Extreme', www.sciencefriday.com, 28 April 2017.

19 Kenneth C. Catania, 'The Sense of Touch in the Star-nosed Mole: From Mechanoreceptors to the Brain', *Philosophical Transactions: Biological Sciences*, CCCLXVI/1581 (12 November 2011), p. 3018.

20 Berry Campbell, 'A Reconsideration of the Shoulder Musculature of the Cape Golden Mole', *Journal of Mammalogy*, XIX/2 (May 1938), p. 239.

21 Michael Stanhope et al., 'Molecular Evidence for Multiple Origins of Insectivora and for a New Order of Endemic African Insectivore Mammals', *Proceedings of the National Academy of Sciences of the United States of America*, LXXXXV/17 (18 August 1998), p. 9971.

22 Matthew J. Mason and Peter M. Narins, 'Seismic Signal Use by Fossorial Mammals', *American Zoologist*, XXXXI/5 (2001), p. 1178.

23 Michael Archer et al., 'Australia's First Fossil Marsupial Mole (Notoryctemorphia) Resolves Controversies about their Evolution and Palaeoenvironmental Origins', *Proceedings: Biological Sciences*, CCLXXVIII/1711 (22 May 2011), p. 1499.

24 Mark S. Springer et al., 'The Interphotoreceptor Retinoid Binding Protein Gene in Therian Mammals: Implications for Higher Level Relationships and Evidence for Loss of Function in the Marsupial Mole', *Proceedings of the National Academy of Sciences of the United States of America*, LXXXXIV/25 (9 December 1997), p. 13758.

25 Mason and Narins, 'Seismic Signal Use by Fossorial Mammals', p. 1178.

26 Archer et al., 'Australia's First Fossil Marsupial Mole', p. 1503.

2 NATURE

1 Gillian Godfrey and Peter Crowcroft, *The Life of the Mole* (London, 1960), p. 115.

2 Rob Atkinson, *Moles* (Stansted, 2013), p. 34.

3 Martyn L. Gorman and R. David Stone, *The Natural History of Moles* (Ithaca, NY, 1990), p. 19; Atkinson, *Moles*, p. 37.

4 Atkinson, *Moles*, p. 26.

5 Gorman and Stone, *Natural History of Moles*, p. 32.

6 Yasushi Yokohata, 'A Brief Review of the Biology on Moles in Japan', *Mammal Study*, XXX (2005), p. S27.

7 Atkinson, *Moles*, p. 30.

8 Godfrey and Crowcroft, *The Life of the Mole*, p. 48.

9 British Mole Catchers Register, 'Albino Moles', www.britishmole catchers.co.uk, accessed 14 May 2018.

10 Yokohata, 'Brief Review of the Biology on Moles in Japan', p. S27.

11 Atkinson, *Moles*, p. 71.

12 Ibid.

13 Ibid., p. 46.

14 Gorman and Stone, *Natural History of Moles*, p. 60.

15 Ibid.

16 Ibid., p. 61.

17 Atkinson, *Moles*, p. 51.

18 Ibid., p. 52.

19 Gorman and Stone, *Natural History of Moles*, p. 69.

20 Ibid., p. 9.

21 Theodore Grand, Edwin Gould and Richard Montali, 'Structure of the Proboscis and Rays of the Star-nosed Mole, *Condylura cristata*', *Journal of Mammalogy*, LXXIX/2 (May 1998), p. 497.

22 Guinness World Records, 'Fastest Eater (Mammals)', www.guinnessworldrecords.com, February 2005.

23 Yolanda Melero, Pere Aymerich, Juan Jose Luque-Larena and Joaquim Gosàlbez, 'New Insights into Social and Space Use Behavior of the Endangered Pyrenean Desman (*Galemys pyrenaicus*)', *European Journal of Wildlife Research*, LVIII (2012), p. 192.

24 Yolanda Melero, Pere Aymerich, G. Santulli and Joaquim Gosàlbez, 'Activity and Space Patterns on Pyrenean Desman (*Galemys pyrenaicus*) Suggest Non-aggressive and Non-territorial Behaviour', *European Journal of Wildlife Research*, LX (2014), pp. 713–14.

25 Anaïs Charbonnel et al., 'Can Recent Global Changes Explain the Dramatic Range Contraction of an Endangered Semi-aquatic Mammal Species in the French Pyrenees?', *PLOS ONE*, XI/7 (2016), p. 11.

26 N. M. Okulova, A. S. Onufrenya and M. V. Onufrenya, 'Analysis of Monitoring Data on the Russian Desman (Desmana Moschata) in the Oka State Biosphere Reserve in Relation to the Problem of Species' Population Decline', *Russian Journal of Ecology*, XXXIX/7 (2008), p. 514.

27 BBC News, 'Russians Rally for Water Mammal', http://news.bbc.co.uk, 9 June 2006.

28 Michael Marshall, 'I'm Pretty and I Don't Know It', *New Scientist*, ccxiii/2849 (28 January 2012).

29 Gorman and Stone, *Natural History of Moles*, p. 7.

30 Samantha Mynhardt et al, 'Phylogeography of a Morphologically Cryptic Golden Mole Assemblage from South-eastern Africa', *plos one*, x/12 (2015), p. 4.

31 U. B. Willi, G. N. Bronner and P. M. Narins, 'Ossicular Differentiation of Airborne and Seismic Stimuli in the Cape Golden Mole (*Chrysochloris asiatica*)', *Journal of Comparative Physiology*, cxcii (2006), p. 276.

32 International Union for Conservation of Nature (iucn) Afrotheria Specialist Group, 'Golden Moles', www.afrotheria.net, accessed 22 May 2018.

33 The Endangered Wildlife Trust, 'Mammal Red List: Order Afrosoricida', www.ewt.org.za, accessed 22 May 2018.

34 Animal Diversity Web, '*Notoryctes typhlops*: Southern Marsupial Mole', https://animaldiversity.org, accessed 22 May 2018.

35 Animal Diversity Web, 'Notoryctemorphia: Marsupial Moles', https://animaldiversity.org, accessed 22 May 2018.

36 Joe Benshemesh, 'The Marsupial Mole: An Enduring Enigma', www.australiangeographic.com.au, 14 September 2010.

37 Kathy Riley, 'Searching for the Marsupial Mole', www.australiangeographic.com.au, 14 September 2010.

38 Joe Benshemesh and Ken Johnson, 'Biology and Conservation of Marsupial Moles (*Notoryctes*)', in *Predators with Pouches: The Biology of Carnivorous Marsupials*, ed. M. Jones, C. Dickman and M. Archer (Collingwood, 2003), p. 472.

3 SCIENTIFIC STUDY

1 T. H. White, ed., *The Book of Beasts* (New York, 1954), pp. 95–6.

2 Ibid., p. 96.

3 'Talpa', *Hortus Sanitatis*, http://cudl.lib.cam.ac.uk, accessed 12 January 2018.

4　Conrad Gessner, *Icones animalium*, www.biodiversitylibrary.org, accessed 12 January 2018.

5　James Madison, 'From James Madison to Thomas Jefferson, 12 May 1786', http://founders.archives.gov, accessed 12 January 2018.

6　Étienne François Dralet, *L'Art du taupier, ou Méthode amusante et infaillible de prendre les taupes* (Paris, 1880), p. 15.

7　Rob Atkinson, *Moles* (Stansted, 2013), pp. 72–3.

8　Dralet, *L'Art du taupier*, p. 40.

9　Gillian Godfrey and Peter Crowcroft, *The Life of the Mole* (London, 1960), p. 52.

10　Martyn L. Gorman and R. David Stone, *The Natural History of Moles* (Ithaca, NY, 1990), p. 65; I.J.H. Lyster, 'Mole Kills Herring Gull', *Scottish Birds*, VII (1972), p. 208.

11　Atkinson, *Moles*, p. 13.

12　Ibid., p. 47.

13　Ibid., p. 122.

14　Mary T. Silcox and Mark F. Teaford, 'The Diet of Worms: An Analysis of Mole Dental Microwear', *Journal of Mammalogy*, LXXXIII/3 (2002), p. 810.

15　James Gorman, 'Uncovering the Secrets of Mole Motion,' www.nytimes.com, 28 January 2014.

16　Ibid.

17　Gorman and Stone, *Natural History of Moles*, p. 38.

18　Kenneth C. Catania, 'Evolution of Brains and Behavior for Optimal Foraging: A Tale of Two Predators', *Proceedings of the National Academy of Sciences of the United States of America*, CIX (26 June 2012), p. 10707.

19　Ibid., p. 10703.

20　Shin-ichiro Kawada, Nguyen Truong Son and Dang Ngoc Can, 'A New Species of Mole of the Genus *Euroscaptor* (Soricomorpha, Talpidae) from Northern Vietnam', *Journal of Mammalogy*, XCIII/3 (2012), pp. 841, 847, 849.

21　5050 Community, 'S8 Ep01 Golden Moles', www.youtube.com, 19 April 2017.

22 Joe Benshemesh, 'Backfilled Tunnels Provide a Novel and Efficient Method of Revealing an Elusive Australian Burrowing Animal', *Journal of Mammalogy*, xcv/5 (2014), p. 1059.

23 Ibid.

4 MOLES IN MYTH AND FOLKLORE

1 Aesop, 'The Mole and His Mother', https://fablesofaesop.com, 16 November 2013.

2 Jean Chevalier and Alain Gheerbrant, *A Dictionary of Symbols*, trans. J. Buchanan-Brown (London, 1996), p. 663.

3 H. Grégoire, R. Goossens and M. Mathieu, 'Asklèpios, Apollon Smintheus et Rudra: Études sur le dieu à la taupe et le dieu au rat dans la Grèce et dans l'Inde', *Académie Royale de Belgique, Classe des Lettres, Mémoires*, xlv/1 (1949).

4 R.S.P. Beekes, *Etymological Dictionary of Greek* (Leiden, 2009), p. xxv.

5 Chevalier and Gheerbrant, *A Dictionary of Symbols*, p. 663.

6 Henry E. Sigerist, *A History of Medicine: Early Greek, Hindu, and Persian Medicine* (New York, 1987), p. 56.

7 Judith Vander, 'The Shoshone Ghost Dance and Numic Myth: Common Heritage, Common Themes', *Journal of California and Great Basin Anthropology*, xvii/2 (1995), p. 179.

8 'Native American Mole Mythology', www.native-languages.org, accessed 13 April 2018.

9 Roland B. Dixon, ed., 'Achomawi Myths', *Journal of American Folk-lore*, xxii/85 (1909), p. 37.

10 'Native American Legends: Spirit Chief Names the Animal People', www.firstpeople.us, accessed 13 April 2018.

11 'Native American Legends: Coyote Quarrels with Mole', www.firstpeople.us, accessed 13 April 2018.

12 H. R. Voth, *The Traditions of the Hopi* (Chicago, il, 1905), p. 314.

13 M. C. Boatright, W. M. Hudson and A. Maxwell, eds, *The Best of Texas Folk and Folklore, 1916–1954* (Denton, tx, 1998), p. 3.

14 James M. Taggart, *Nahuat Myth and Social Structure* (Austin, tx, 1997), p. 222.

15 George Schwab, 'Bulu-Folk-tales', *Journal of American Folk-lore*, XXVII (1914), p. 276.

16 Zinta Konrad, *Ewe Comic Heroes: Trickster Tales in Togo* (Abingdon and New York, 2015), p. 200.

17 Patricia Ann Lynch, *African Mythology A to Z* (New York, 2004), p. 71.

18 Joe Benshemesh and Ken Johnson, 'Biology and Conservation of Marsupial Moles (*Notoryctes*)', in *Predators with Pouches: The Biology of Carnivorous Marsupials*, ed. M. Jones, C. Dickman and M. Archer (Collingwood, 2003), p. 465.

19 John Pickrell, 'A Desert-dwelling Enigma', *Australian Geographic*, 116 (September/October 2013).

20 Parks Australia, 'Mammals Fact Sheet: Uluru-Kata Tjuta National Park', https://parksaustralia.gov.au, accessed 3 July 2018.

21 Krisztina Turza, 'Uluru Excursion, Northern Territory, AU', www.turzart.com, July 2013.

22 Benshemesh and Johnson, 'Biology and Conservation of Marsupial Moles', p. 472.

23 See Robert E. Bieder, *Bear* (London, 2005), pp. 56, 77.

24 John Batchelor, *The Ainu and Their Folk-lore* (London, 1901), p. 262.

25 Ibid.

26 Ibid.

27 Ibid., p. 501.

28 Ibid., p. 502.

29 Ibid.

30 Ibid., p. 503.

31 Basil Hall Chamberlain, *Aino Folk-tales* (Saxony, 1888), p. 15.

32 Ibid.

33 See Martin Wallen, *Fox* (London, 2006), pp. 60–69.

34 Robin D. Gill, *Rise, Ye Sea Slugs! 1,000 Holothurian Haiku* (Key Biscayne, FL, 2003), p. 109.

35 Ibid., p. 195.

36 See Chapter One.

37 Gill, *Rise, Ye Sea Slugs!*, p. 197.

38 Alethea Helbig and Agnes Perkins, *This Land is Our Land: A Guide to Multicultural Literature for Children and Young Adults* (Westport, CT, 1994), p. 159.

39 Admiel Kosman, 'Heaven, the Mole and the Well: A Study of a Talmudic Theological Concept', *European Judaism*, XLVI/2 (2013), p. 101.

40 Ibid., pp. 106, 107.

41 Josepha Sherman, *Mythology for Storytellers: Themes and Tales from Around the World* (London and New York, 2015), p. 40.

42 Ibid.

43 Friedrich Nietzsche, *Thus Spoke Zarathustra*, trans. Walter Kaufmann (New York, 1966), p. 198.

44 Richard Dehmel, 'Das Märchen vom Maulwurf', gutenberg. spiegel.de, accessed 22 May 2018.

45 Ibid.

46 Wil Huygen and Rien Poortvliet, *Gnomes* (New York, 1976), p. 61.

47 Hans Christian Andersen, *The Complete Fairy Tales and Stories* (New York, 1974), p. 35.

48 IMDb, 'Barry Manilow: Awards', www.imdb.com, accessed 14 May 2018

49 Barry Mahon and R. Winer, dirs, *RiffTrax: Santa and the Ice Cream Bunny*, Legend Films (2010).

50 Rob Atkinson, *Moles* (Stansted, 2013), p. 113; Robert Stephen Hawker, *Footprints of Former Men in Far Cornwall* (London, 1903), p. 27.

51 Ibid., p. 30.

52 Ibid., p. 31.

53 J. P. Schinhan, ed., *North Carolina Folklore*, vol. V (Durham, NC, 1962), p. 126.

54 W. H. Babcock, 'Mole-lore', *Science*, IX/220 (22 April 1887), p. 389.

55 Ibid., pp. 389–90.

56 Kate Stockton Kelley, 'Betsey and the Mole Skin', in *American Myths, Legends, and Tall Tales: An Encyclopedia of American Folklore*, vol. I: *A–F*, ed. C. R. Fee and J. B. Webb (Santa Barbara, CA, and Denver, CO, 2016), p. 107.

57 Ibid.
58 Ibid.
59 Ibid.
60 Vance Randolph, *Ozark Magic and Folklore* (New York, 1947), p. 155.
61 Science Museum, 'Mole's Foot Amulet, Norfolk, England, 1890–1910', http://broughttolife.sciencemuseum.org.uk, accessed 13 April 2018.
62 Babcock, 'Mole-lore', p. 389.
63 C. L. Daniels and C. M. Stevans, eds, *Encyclopaedia of Superstitions, Folklore, and the Occult Sciences of the World* (Chicago, IL, and Milwaukee, WI, 1903), vol. III, pp. 1670–71.
64 Ibid., p. 1675.

5 ALLEGORICAL MOLES

1 C. G. Jung, *Dream Analysis: Notes of the Seminar Given in 1928–1930* (Princeton, NJ, 1984), p. 514.
2 'Queen Alexandra and Moleskins', *Cloaks and Furs*, XXXIII/9 (April 1904), p. 56.
3 Étienne François Dralet, *L'Art du taupier, ou Méthode amusante et infaillible de prendre les taupes* (Paris, 1880), p. 112.
4 Matt Sebra, 'Moleskin: Your Fall Fabric Middleweight Champion', www.gq.com, 5 October 2012.
5 Young Lee, 'Digging into Moleskin – Textile Tales', www.heddels.com, 25 April 2015.
6 Hector Tobar, 'Buy a Moleskine Notebook, Build an Empire', http://articles.latimes.com, 12 March 2013.
7 John le Carré, *Tinker Tailor Soldier Spy* (London, 1974), p. 62.
8 Steven Erlanger, 'Kim Philby, Lecturing in East Berlin in '81, Bragged of How Easy It Was to Fool MI6', www.nytimes.com, 4 April 2016.
9 Ibid.
10 William Hood, *Mole* (New York, 1982), p. 16.
11 David A. Vise, *The Bureau and the Mole* (New York, 2002), pp. 65, 165.
12 Ibid., p. 165.

13 Greg Kot, 'Living in Oblivion: A Flaming Lip Interviews the Mole Man', http://articles.chicagotribune.com, 14 June 1996.

14 In Ashokamitran, *Mole!* (New Delhi, 2005), pp. 160–61.

15 Margaret Christoph, 'Mole Day', *Science Teacher*, LII/7 (October 1985), p. 48.

16 J.J.N. Palmer, 'Place: Molesworth', http://opendomesday.org, accessed 14 June 2018.

17 BBC News, 'RAF Mildenhall, Alconbury and Molesworth among MOD sites to be sold', www.bbc.com, 18 January 2016.

18 ARTY Net, '"Tom" Daniel's B/2/77FA "Mole City" Album for 1969', http://277arty.net, accessed 14 June 2018.

19 Ron Leonard, 'Battle of FSB Mole City Information', www.vhpa.org, 24 September 2017.

20 4/9 Infantry Manchu Association, 'Mole City: 1968–69', www.manchu.org, accessed 14 May 2018.

21 John Senka, 'Manchus at Mole City', www.manchu.org, accessed 14 May 2018.

22 Anthony Taille, 'The Truth about New York's Legendary "Mole People"', http://narrative.ly, 29 October 2015.

23 Jennifer Toth, *The Mole People: Life in the Tunnels beneath New York City* (Chicago, IL, 1993), p. ix.

24 Ibid.

25 Ibid., p. 39.

26 Ibid., p. x.

27 Taille, 'The Truth about New York's Legendary "Mole People"'.

6 MOLES IN LITERARY AND POPULAR CULTURE

1 William Blake, 'The Book of Thel', in *The Complete Poetry and Prose of William Blake*, ed. David Erdman (Berkeley, CA, 2008), p. 3.

2 Theodore Roethke, 'The Pit', in *The Collected Poems of Theodore Roethke* (New York, 1975), p. 52.

3 Jay Parini, 'Blake and Roethke: When Everything Comes to One', in *William Blake and the Moderns*, ed. R. J. Bertholf and A. S. Levitt (Albany, NY, 1982), p. 76.

4 Jenijoy La Belle, *The Echoing Wood of Theodore Roethke* (Princeton, NJ, 1976), p. 93.

5 Roethke, 'The Abyss', in *Collected Poems of Theodore Roethke*, p. 212.

6 Alejandro Jodorowsky, dir., *El Topo*, Producciones Pánicas (1970).

7 Roger Ebert, 'El Topo', www.rogerebert.com, 6 October 2007.

8 Quoted in Thomas Lash, 'Publishing: Moles Have Their Day', *New York Times* (23 November 1979), p. 28.

9 Ash Silverlock, 'An Interview with William Horwood', ashsilverlock.com, 19 February 2017.

10 James Hillman, *Animal Presences* (Putnam, CT, 2008), p. 173.

11 Ibid., p. 174.

12 William Horwood, *Duncton Wood* (New York, 1980), p. 61.

13 William Horwood, *Duncton Stone* (London, 1993), p. 691.

14 Unsubject, 'Three Decades of Monty Mole', https://unsubject. wordpress.com, 10 January 2015.

15 Andrew Young, 'A Dead Mole', in *Selected Poems* (Manchester, 1998), p. 75.

16 Sylvia Plath, 'Blue Moles', in *The Collected Poems*, ed. Ted Hughes (New York, 1992), p. 126.

17 Sylvia Plath, *The Journals of Sylvia Plath* (New York, 1998), p. 324.

18 Plath, 'Blue Moles', p. 126.

19 Ibid.

20 Ibid.

21 Anne Sexton, *The Complete Poems* (Boston, MA, 1999), p. 497.

22 Anne Sexton, 'Star-nosed Mole', in *The Complete Poems* (Boston, MA, 1999), p. 500.

23 Ibid.

24 Ibid.

25 Seamus Heaney, 'Bone Dreams', in *North* (London, 1975), p. 23.

26 Ibid.

27 Ibid.

28 Ibid.

29 Raphaël Ingelbien, *Misreading England: Poetry and Nationhood since the Second World War* (Amsterdam and New York, 2002), p. 176.

30 Graham Mort, 'Mole Totem', in *Snow from the North* (Sydney, 1992), p. 30.

31 Ibid.

32 Mary Oliver, 'The Summer Day', in *Devotions* (New York, 2017), p. 316.

33 Mary Oliver, 'Moles', in *American Primitive* (Boston, MA, and New York, 1983), p. 10.

34 Ibid.

35 Ibid., p. 11.

36 Ted Hughes, 'Mole', in *Collected Poems for Children* (New York, 2005), p. 23.

37 D. H. Lawrence, 'Second Best', in *The Complete Stories of D. H. Lawrence* (Pickering, 2007), p. 173.

38 Franz Kafka, *Letters to Friends, Family, and Editors*, trans. Richard and Clara Winston (New York, 1977), p. 17.

39 Franz Kafka, *The Complete Stories*, ed. Nahum N. Glatzer (New York, 1995), p. 169.

40 Ibid., p. 352.

41 Éric Chevillard, 'Moles', trans. Alyson Waters, *Common Knowledge*, XXI/1 (2015), p. 139.

42 Kenneth Grahame, *The Wind in the Willows* (New York, 2005), p. 69.

43 Ibid., p. 66.

44 Seth Lehrer, 'Style and the Mole: Domestic Aesthetics in "The Wind in the Willows"', *Journal of Aesthetic Education*, XLIII/2 (Summer 2009), p. 59.

45 Grahame, *The Wind in the Willows*, p. 67.

46 Ibid., p. 3.

47 Ibid., p. 170.

48 Ibid., p. 168.

49 Quoted in Albert Borden Stridsberg, 'On Illustrating Kenneth Grahame', *Yale University Library Gazette*, XXIV/1 (July 1949), p. 33.

50 Ibid., p. 34.

51 Wes Anderson, dir., *Fantastic Mr Fox*, 20th Century Fox and Indian Paintbrush (2009).

52 Dennis Hevesi, 'Zdenek Miler, Creator of Krtek the Mole, Dies at 90', www.nytimes.com, 2 December 2011.

53 Ibid.

54 Philip J. Heijmans, 'Communism's Answer to Mickey Mouse is Thrust into a Very Capitalist Dispute', www.nytimes.com, 23 October 2017.

55 Doreen Carvajal, 'No Wizards, Matey, They're Wise Enoof; A Gritty Liverpudlian Finds Refuge with Feisty Woodland Critters', www.nytimes.com, 2 April 2001.

56 Colin Meloy, *Under Wildwood* (New York, 2012), p. 379.

57 Josh Stillman, 'The Decemberists' Colin Meloy on "Under Wildwood"', www.ew.com, 25 September 2012.

58 Clara Dillingham Pierson, *Among the Forest People* (New York, 1898), p. 174.

59 Arthur Scott Bailey, *The Tale of Grandfather Mole* (New York, 1920), p. 100.

60 Ibid., p. 120.

61 Thornton W. Burgess, *Mother West Wind 'Why' Stories* (Boston, MA, 1915), pp. 120–21.

62 Ibid., p. 128.

63 Lee Sholem, dir., *Superman and the Mole-men*, Lippert Pictures (1951).

64 John Byrne, *The Sensational She-Hulk*, II/33 (New York, November 1991), p. 27.

65 Jim Mallon, dir., *Mystery Science Theater 3000: Mole People*, series 8, episode 3 (1997).

66 Antonio Leonviola, dir., *Mole Men against the Son of Hercules*, Leone Film (1961).

67 John Hodgman, *More Information than You Require* (New York, 2008), p. 569.

68 Ibid., p. 555.

69 '700 Mole-men', www.flickr.com, 18 March 2007.

70 James Edmunds, dir., *The Molers*, Luminoid Films (2013).

1 James Anderson, 'The Mole', *The Bee, or Literary Weekly Intelligencer*, II (1791), p. 98.
2 Ibid., p. 99.
3 Ibid.
4 Brendan Borrell, 'Going Underground: Inside the World of the Mole-catchers', www.theguardian.com, 8 March 2017.
5 Jeff Nicholls, *Catching Moles: The History and Practice* (Ramsbury, 2017), p. 50.
6 Borrell, 'Going Underground'.
7 Frances Hubbard, 'Louise Used to be a Drama Teacher. Now She Kills Moles', www.telegraph.co.uk, 18 April 2015.
8 Jeff Nicholls, *Mole Catching: A Practical Guide* (Ramsbury, 2008), p. 8.
9 Nicholls, *Catching Moles*, p. 27.
10 Ibid., p. 29.
11 Ibid., p. 45.
12 Martyn L. Gorman and R. David Stone, *The Natural History of Moles* (Ithaca, NY, 1990), pp. 105–6.
13 Susan E. Baker et al, 'Moles and Mole Control on British Farms, Amenities and Gardens after Strychnine Withdrawal', *Animals*, VI/6 (2016), p. 26.
14 Nicholls, *Catching Moles*, p. 171.
15 Hubbard, 'Louise Used to be a Drama Teacher'.
16 John Clare, 'The Mole-catcher', in *English Verse, 1830–1890*, ed. Bernard Richards (Abingdon, 1999), p. 14.
17 Ibid.
18 Ibid., p. 15.
19 Hubbard, 'Louise Used to be a Drama Teacher'.
20 Neanda Salvaterra, 'England Has a Mole Problem: Feuding Mole Catchers', www.wsj.com, 13 November 2016.
21 Borrell, 'Going Underground'.
22 Gorman and Stone, *Natural History of Moles*, p. 15.
23 Hubbard, 'Louise Used to be a Drama Teacher'.

24 Josh Morris, 'Mole-catcher Defends Denbigh Moors Display of Dead Animals', www.dailypost.co.uk, 30 January 2015.

25 George Saunders, 'The Semplica-girl Diaries', *New Yorker* (15 October 2012), p. 75.

26 International Arcade Museum, 'WhacAMole', www.arcade-museum.com, accessed 3 July 2018.

27 'A Man who Made Whac-A-Mole' [in Japanese], www.chibarei. blog.jp (1996), accessed 3 July 2018.

28 E-mail to author, 31 August 2016.

29 Luca Chittaro and Riccardo Sioni, 'Killing Non-human Animals in Video Games: A Study on User Experience and Desensitization to Violence Aspects', *PsychNology Journal*, x/3 (2012), p. 215.

30 Ibid., p. 238.

31 E-mail to author, 31 August 2016.

32 Patrick Barkham, 'Don't Moles Have a Right to Life Too?', www.theguardian.com, 22 February 2016.

33 Mark Cocker, 'Country Diary: We Have Reached an Arrangement with Our Mole', www.theguardian.com, 4 January 2018.

Select Bibliography

Atkinson, Rob, *Moles* (Stansted, 2013)

Godfrey, Gillian, and Peter Crowcroft, *The Life of the Mole* (London, 1960)

Gorman, Martyn L., and R. David Stone, *The Natural History of Moles* (Ithaca, NY, 1990)

Grahame, Kenneth, *The Wind in the Willows* (London, 1908)

Hamer, Marc, *How to Catch a Mole and Find Yourself in Nature* (London, 2019)

Horwood, William, *Duncton Found* (London, 1989)

—, *Duncton Quest* (London, 1988)

—, *Duncton Rising* (London, 1992)

—, *Duncton Stone* (London, 1993)

—, *Duncton Tales* (London, 1991)

—, *Duncton Wood* (London, 1980)

Mellanby, Kenneth, *The Mole* (New York, 1971)

Nicholls, Jeff, *Catching Moles: The History and Practice* (Ramsbury, 2017)

—, *Mole Catching: A Practical Guide* (Ramsbury, 2008)

Randell, Arthur, *Fenland Molecatcher* (Abingdon, 1970)

Stone, David, *Moles* (Oswestry, 1986)

Stone, R. David, *The Mole* (London, 1999)

Associations and Websites

ASSOCIATION OF PROFESSIONAL MOLE CATCHERS
www.associationofprofessionalmolecatchers.org

THE BRITISH MOLE CATCHERS REGISTER
www.britishmolecatchers.co.uk

THE GUILD OF BRITISH MOLECATCHERS
www.guildofbritishmolecatchers.co.uk

Acknowledgements

This book is dedicated to Kay and Tom Ellerhoff. I am grateful for their support, which included their attendance at my commencements at Trinity College, Dublin. Their lifelong commitment to wildlife, made both professionally and personally, set the bar for which this book was written. Love you, AK and Unca Tom!

Thanks also to my parents, my sister, Arion, and Yael. Big thanks to Nick, Sally and Malena Villegas-Moore, who welcomed me back to Oregon while this book was wrapping up. Kevin, Alaina, Alexander and Theodore Storrar, thank you for our friendship – and for taking me to Belas Knap Long Barrow, where we found stone-riddled molehills atop the ancient monument. Love also to Francesca and John Storrar, who gave me, Jackie and Issy a tour of the Wirral's finest molehills.

I wish to thank all the people who, while I wrote this book, kept bringing moles to my attention. I am particularly indebted to those who provided sources that made their way into the book: Catherine Rihm at Beaverdale Books, Philip Coleman, Melanie Otto, Amanda Piesse, Brendan O'Connell, Linda Gronert, Sorrel Brown, Michael Morris, Alecs Mickunas, Shin-ichiro Kawada, Jessica Molina, Mark Sherinian, Jane McMillan, Jessica Milazzo, Allyson Hermann, Miranda Corcoran and Sara Snyder. My gratitude extends to Michael Leaman, Jonathan Burt and Phoebe Colley, whose attention and graciousness made this a better book.

A sincere thank you, as well, to Louise Chapman, Norfolk's very own Lady Mole Catcher® and head of the British Mole Catchers Register, for allowing me to shadow her at work, answering all of my questions and being generous with her time.

Photo Acknowledgements

The author and the publishers wish to express their thanks to the below sources of illustrative material and/or permission to reproduce it.

Reproduced with permission of Alexei Abramov: p. 69; Mark Anderson: p. 103; Christian Anke: pp. 105, 123; Author's photos: pp. 6, 22, 24, 28, 51, 106, 109, 121, 129, 174, 175; Ayre & Co.: p. 102; David Bleasdale: p. 178; Bert Cash: p. 37; Kirt Edblom: p. 181; Reproduced with permission of James Edmunds and Luminoid Films: p. 154; Martyn Fletcher: p. 34; GalleryofHope: p. 29; Gillian Godfrey: p. 62; Helfrich: pp. 41, 42; Amanda Hillbraith: p. 67; Sam Howzit: p.182; Reproduced with permission of Shin-ichiro Kawada: p. 68; Joost Makerink: p. 159; R. Crap Mariner: p. 135; The Metropolitan Museum of Art, New York: p. 100 (Gift of Mrs John C. Tomlinson, 1965); Reproduced with permission of Jessica Milazzo: p. 81; Michael Mol: p. 40; Nalnoc: p. 186; © National Comics Publications (1951): p. 146; Jjacek Loco Pocos (2014): p. 120; Reproduced with permission of Tim Randall © 2010: p. 48; Babarczl Reka: p. 140; Rachel Semlyen: p. 30; Steve p2008 (2001): p. 111; Reproduced with permission of Kevin Storrar: p. 75; The Ian Taylor: p. 125; Jean-Christophe Theil: p. 10; Paolo Trabattoni: p. 99; Robert Trevis-Smith: p. 26; Image © Universal Pictures Co.: pp. 149, 151; Andrlus Vanagas : p. 138; WzimuO: p. 183; Wuppertal: p. 157; Zenera: p. 35; Brendan Zim: p. 160; Paul Zimmer: p. 152.

Index

Page numbers in *italics* refer to illustrations

Aberdeen Bestiary *56*
Aesop 72, *73*, 82
albino moles 32–3, *33*, *121*
Alexandra, queen
    of Denmark 100, 188
Almond, Marc 65
Ames, Aldrich 105
Andersen, Hans Christian
    89–91, 136
Anderson, Wes 136
Aristotle 7–8
Asclepius 73–4
Ashmole Bestiary *54*
Ashokamitran 106–7
Association of Professional
    Mole Catchers 176
Atkinson, Rob 35, 58, 64–5,
    92, 178
Audubon, John James *64*
Australian Department of Parks
    and Wildlife 52
Avogadro, Amedeo *107*, 108

Bailey, Arthur Scott, *The Tale
    of Grandfather Mole* 142–4

Barnhart, Nancy, *Wind in the
    Willows 133*, 134
Beckett, Samuel 129, 131
Benshemesh, Joe 51, 71, 78
Blake, William, 'Thel's Motto'
    114–15, 123, 137
blind mole 27
blindness 8, 23–4, 27, 45,
    49, 53–4, 72, 79, 83,
    88–9, 98, 113, 115, 122,
    136, 156
Bluth, Don 90
Bracquemond, Felix, *Les Taupes
    170*
Bransom, Paul, *Wind in the
    Willows 130*, 134
British Mole Catchers Register
    (BMCR) 175–6
Burgess, Thornton W. 144

Caliban 113
Cape mole *21*, *46*, 47
Catania, Kenneth 18–19, 67
cats 80–82
Channing, Carol 91

Chapman, Louise 166–8, 172–6, *174*, *175*, 178–80
Chatwin, Bruce 101
chemistry 107–8
Chevillard, Éric, 'Moles' 127, 129, 131
Clare, John, 'The Mole-catcher' 176
coast moles 65
Congo golden mole 78
Coyote (trickster) 74–6

Dahl, Roald 136
Darwin, Charles 9–11
Davies, Richard 106
De Winton's golden mole 48
dead-mole poets 121–6
Dehmel, Richard, 'Das Märchen vom Maulwurf' 87–8
desmans 12, 42–4, *43*, *44*
Dickies, The (band) 151
Disney 90, 131, 134, *135*, 139
Dralet, Étienne François 57–8, 61
Duffus, John 171, 189
Duncton Wood (novel) 118–20, 135, 141, 189

earthworms 31, 34–6, 47, 65–6, 119
eastern mole *37*, 65
Ebert, Roger 117
Ehlert, Lois, *Mole's Hill* 137–8
Eimer's organs 18–19, 40–41, 43, 123, 156
El Topo (film) 115–18, *116*

Endangered Wildlife Trust of South Africa 48, 70
enlightenment 118, 138
Eotalpa 12, 188
Eremitalpa 23, 24
espionage 102–7
Etchells, Frederick, *The Dead Mole* 127
European mole *13*, *14*, *17*, *26*, 28, 29, 30, *34*, *35*, 36–7, 39, 55, 58, *59*, *61*, 62–4, *85*, 99
Euroscaptor orlovi 69
Euroscaptor subanura 69

Fantastic Mr Fox (film) 136
Fechter, Aaron 182–4
field mouse 89–91, *92*, *93*
folk medicine 54, 96–7
fortress 30–32, *31*, *32*
foxes 50, 80–82, 122, 137, 180

Gessner, Conrad, *Talpa* 55, *58*
giant golden mole 45
Gill, Robin D. 83–4
Gnomes (book) 89
Godfrey, Gillian 31, 58, 61–3, *62*, 189
golden moles 19–23, *22*, 45–9, *46*, *48*, 50, 69–71, 78, *78*,
Gorman, Martyn L. 28, 37, 40, 63–4, 66, 179
Grahame, Kenneth 131–5, 136, 188
Guild of British Molecatchers 176
Guinness World Records 41, 189

hairy-tailed moles *64*, 65–6
Hamilton, James 136
Hamlet 113
Hanssen, Robert Philip 104
Hardy, Thomas *129*
Hawker, Robert Stephen,
    'The First Cornish Mole' 92
Heaney, Seamus, 'Bone Dreams'
    124
hedgehogs 12, *13*, *85*, *121*
Hemingway, Ernest 101
Henry iv, Part 1 114
Hillman, James 118
Hodgman, John 152–3
Hollar, Wenceslaus *61*
Hortus sanitatis 54, *57*
Horwood, William 118–20, 135,
    137, 141, 189
Hottentot golden mole 46
Howitt, Samuel, *Ass, Ape and*
    Mole 73
Huet, Joseph, *Congo golden mole*
    78
Hughes, Ted 122, 124, 126
Hurt, John 90

Imaizumi, Yoshiharu 34–5, 68
Isaiah 7
itjaritjari 23, 49, 52, 71, 78
    see also marsupial moles

Jacques, Brian 141–2
Janosch 136–7
Japanese mountain mole 15
Jarvis, *Mrs Mole, I'm Home!* 137

Jefferson, Thomas 56
Jesus 76–7
Jodorowsky, Alejandro 115–18,
    137
Jung, C. G. 98

Kafka, Franz 87, 127, 128–9, 131
kakarratul 23, 49, 52, 78
    see also marsupial moles
Kawada, Shin-ichiro 68, 69
Kettle, Stephen *125*
Key, Vanessa Terrell, *Queenie of*
    the Hill 156
Krtek *123*, *138*, 138–41, *140*, *152*,
    189

Lawrence, D. H. 127, 131
Le Carré, John 102, 104, 188
Leclerc, Georges-Louis, comte de
    Buffon *16*, *21*, 55–6, *59*, *60*
Lin, Yi-Fen 65
Linnaeus, Carl 69
Lorrie, Peter 102
luck charms 79, 96–7, *96*

Madison, James 56
Manilow, Barry 91
marriage 7, 72, 80, 85–6, 89–91,
    94, 127, 147
marsupial moles 19, 23–5, *23*, *24*,
    49–52, *51*, 69, *70*, 71, 78–9, 188
Milazzo, Jessica, *Mole 81*
Miler, Zdeněk 139, 189
Milne, A. A. 133–4
Minogue, Kylie 65

Minyma Itjaritjari (Marsupial
    Mole Woman) 78–9
Mireuk, The 84–5
Mogera 30
Mole (character)
    Ainu 79–82
    Apache 76
    Ewe 77
    Romanian 86–7
    Wind in the Willows 130, 131–5,
    133, *135*
Mole and Troll (book) 135
mole-catchers 33, 38, 57, 124, *162*,
    163, 164–80, *165*, *166*, *173*, *174*,
    175, *177*, 189
Mole City 109–11, *110*, 188
Mole Day 108
mole exorcism 83
'Mole in the Hole, The' (song)
    156–7
Mole Man (Marvel comics) 147–8
mole men 144–156
*Mole Men against the Son of
    Hercules* (film) 150–51
Mole People, The (band) 151–2
Mole People, The (film) 148–51,
    148, *150*, *151*, 189
mole people (pejorative) 111–12,
    153
mole rat 42, 46
molehills 6, 27–8, *28*, *30*, 31, 61,
    73, 83, 99, 108, 113, 121, *129*,
    137, 144, 156, *159*, 161–2,
    167, 172, 179–80, 184, 185,
    186, 188

Moleman of Belmont Avenue (film)
    153, 155
Molers, The (film) 153–5, *154*
Moles, The (band) 106
moleskin 50, 95–6, *100*, 100–101,
    112, 188
Moleskine 101
Molesworth 108, *109*
Morocco Mole 102, *103*
Mort, Graham, 'Mole Totem'
    124–5, 179
mouldwarp 99, 114
Murungu (Meru Supreme God)
    77–8
Mû'yi (Hopi character) 76
Mystery Science Theater 3000
    (TV series) 150

naked mole rats 42
Nicholls, Jeff 164, 169–70, 178
Nietzsche, Friedrich 87

Oliver, Mary, 'Moles' 126
Oreotalpa florissantensis 15,
    188
Owens, Richard *14*

Paley, William 9
Philby, Kim 104
Picasso, Pablo 101
Pierson, Clara Dillingham,
    'The Quarrelsome Mole'
    142
Plath, Sylvia, 'Blue Moles' 122
Plato 138

Popov, Major Pyotr 104
Pul'-laqu-whu (Mole, the Mound
    Digger) 74–5

Rackham, Arthur 134
radio-tracking 37, 43, 63–4
radioactive-tracking 61–3, 189
RAF Molesworth 108
Reeves, George 145, *146*
Reynard the Fox 87, *88*
RiffTrax 91
Roethke, Theodore 115, 122–3, 137
Royal Society for the Prevention
    of Cruelty to Animals (RSPCA)
    179–80
Rudra 74
Ryukyu mole 16

Saint-Hilaire, Geoffroy 58, 61
Santa and the Ice Cream Bunny
    (film) 91
Saul of the Mole People (TV series)
    152
Saunders, George 181–2
sea slugs 83–4
Second Life *120, 121*
Senkaku mole 16
Sexton, Anne, 'Star-nosed Mole'
    122–4
Shakespeare, William 113–14
Shayne, C. C. *100*
Shepard, E. H. 134
Shirt Tales (cartoon) 136
shrew moles 12
shrews 12

Siberian mole *20*
Skinned in the Willows (novelette)
    75
small Japanese mole 34–5
Smith, Harry L., *Grandfather
    Mole* 142, *143*
Socrates 97
Southlanders, The (band) 156–7
spiritual questing 8, 72, 74, 86,
    115, 117–18, 137
star-nosed mole *18*, 18–19, *21*,
    39–41, *41, 42*, 56, *60*, 66–7, *67,
    120*, 122–4, 189
Stone, R. David 28, 37, 40, 63–4,
    66, 179
Storrar, Kevin, *Crime Officer
    Mole 75*
*Story of the Little Mole Who Went
    in Search of Whodunit, The*
    (book) 137
strychnine 172, 189
Stuhlman's golden mole 78
Superman and the Mole Men (film)
    145–7, *146*

Talpa 12, 13, 53, 100
taupe 100–101
Thumbelina 89–91, *92, 93*, 136
Thumbelina (film) 90–91
Topo Chico 185
Topographia Hiberniae 54
Toth, Jennifer 111–12
Townsend's mole 27
transformation into mole 84,
    94–5, 115, 122, 147

traps 168–174, *169, 173, 174*, 189
tunnels 7, 16, 27–31, 35–9, 41, 46,
     49, 51, 61–3, 66, 71, 76–7, 90,
     99, 111–12, 115, 117, 119, 128,
     144, 146, 152, 159–62, *160*,
     168–75, 180

Uttley, Alison 137

Van Gogh, Vincent 101
Vine, John, *Celebrated Kentish
     and Surrey Molecatcher 163*
Vise, David A. 104

Walters, James Lewis, *Llanboidy
     Mole Catcher 166*
Wanted: Monty Mole (video
     game) 120, 189
Washington, George 101
Wells, H. G. 145
Whac-A-Mole 180–84, *181, 182*,
     188
White, T. H. 53
Wildwood Chronicles, The (book
     series) 141–2
William III, king of England 179,
     188
Wind in the Willows, The (book)
     130, 131–5, *133, 135*, 188

Yaccarino, Dan, *Morris Mole* 138
Yoshida, Kazuo 182
Young, Andrew, 'A Dead Mole'
     121–2